...Kean's life itself is a journey of adventure. She tells her ... lively and engaging style and along the way she creates ...story for our time. It is an inspiring narrative of search and ...very; narrative of an inner journey of the soul as well as an ...ter journey in the world.
...atish Kumar, Editor-in-Chief, *Resurgence & Ecologist*

Mags MacKean is one of those rare LionHearted individuals who's particular brand of fearlessness is achieved by love and reverence for Creation. Her adventures will encourage others to take responsibility for their own shadows and recreate their worlds for the better, just as she leaves her own unique paw print in support of Mother Nature.
Linda Tucker, best-selling author & founder, The Global White Lion Protection Trust

Join Mags MacKean for an extraordinary adventure that will leave you seeing your own amazing life in a whole new light.
Tim Freke, philosopher and author of *The Mystery Experience*

Loved Mags MacKean's wonderful work of self-discovery, exploration and awakening. I feel such a kinship with this fellow seeker, whom I am honoured to call 'friend'. Her work is profound and eloquent... and it will move you.
Patricia Cori, bestselling author

Mags MacKea... ...powerful and compelling jou... ...around my shoulders, lon... ...whispers of

snarling ghouls. This is a book about co[...]
soul-cry of a woman who chooses to plung[...]
wondrous life, and find her way. I walk alongsi[...]
Mac Macartney, Embercombe founder, author, spea[...]

The Upside Down Mountain

best wishes,
Mags MacKean

The Upside Down Mountain

Mags MacKean

BOOKS

Winchester, UK
Washington, USA

First published by O-Books, 2016
O-Books is an imprint of John Hunt Publishing Ltd., Laurel House, Station Approach,
Alresford, Hants, SO24 9JH, UK
office1@jhpbooks.net
www.johnhuntpublishing.com

For distributor details and how to order please visit the 'Ordering' section on our website.

Text copyright: Mags MacKean 2015

ISBN: 978 1 78535 171 6
Library of Congress Control Number: 2015941053

A CIP catalogue record for this book is available from the British Library.

Design: Stuart Davies

Printed and bound by CPI Group (UK) Ltd, Croydon, CR0 4YY, UK

We operate a distinctive and ethical publishing philosophy in all
areas of our business, from our global network of authors to
production and worldwide distribution.

CONTENTS

Praise for *Meetings On the Edge: A High-level Escape from Office Routine*

The In Pinn, Neil Wilson Publishing Ltd

Brave, witty and inspiring: Mags MacKean has written a fine book about swapping life at the office desk for life on the mountain ridge.

Robert Macfarlane, author of *Mountains of the Mind*

Mags is simply one of life's braves!
Bear Grylls, adventurer

Everybody dreams it but Mags MacKean has done it – turned her back on the office and climbed mountains instead... it fast became clear she had seen and loved just the same Pyrenees as I have.

Matthew Parris, writer and broadcaster

Acknowledgements

The Upside Down Mountain has had multiple reinventions. As I tried to keep faithful to my memory of events, present day challenges erupted along the way. It was as if the spirit of the book was testing the authenticity of my 'descent' as well as my resolve to live its wisdom. As unexpected circumstances threatened to eclipse the history I was writing about, a word, phrase or sentence would stand out for no longer being a truthful record of my experience. There is a gulf I've had to face between theory and practice.

I owe the transformation of *The Upside Down Mountain*, and its publication, to the dogged faith and scrutiny of my American editor Neva Welton. My thanks too to John Hunt of John Hunt Publishing, who was willing to reconsider the manuscript after its significant reworking.

Thank you for the help and advice of Barbara Turner Vesselago who mentored me during early experimental drafts. And, David Holford, Michael Weiss and Geraldine Overton for their encouragement and shrewd feedback in the opening sections.

Writing is often regarded as a solitary occupation. In this I am fortunate – drawing on the support of friends, family, and creative community in Bristol and the South West where I am blessed to live.

Gravity's Law
How surely gravity's law,
strong as an ocean current,
takes hold of the smallest thing
and pulls it toward the heart of the world.
Each thing –
each stone, blossom, child –
is held in place.
– Rainer Maria Rilke

Preface

Stories. They stalk us. And we stalk them. Bound by their spell and identified with them, they are friends or foes, signposting the way to joy or fear. As one version liberates, another imprisons. While we revel in the fictional tales around us, believing in their power, we often don't realise how life itself is a story we co-create.

I've always liked telling stories. As a child I'd spend hours briefing rows of dolls and furry animals about the twisting fortunes of everything that shaped my young world. Recounting everyday details helped me make sense of my experience. With my audience's mute encouragement, I discovered a parallel world real for being imagined: mythical landscapes and creatures, magical powers rewarding brave escapes from demonic captors, adventures on stormy seas in leaking boats. Storytelling opened up another dimension within myself, as alive as the physical world to which I belonged. But unlike the dense matter of my everyday reality, as a storyteller I could steer the outcomes with a tweak in vision, a shift in focus, a change to even a minor detail.

The freedom I felt in my imaginal realm did not extend to the more serious business of growing up and navigating my own real life drama. The world could be so frustratingly ordinary, so difficult, lonely and sad. Where my imaginary heroine could cleave the life she wanted through her own free will, I struggled to keep true to my own spirited nature. It was more comfortable to fit in, and adopt the dominant narrative of my peers, family and employers. Personal success was a measure of my self-worth. Purpose was in ascending the ladder of hopes and dreams. I was invested in 'tomorrow', a horizon promising my arrival. Happiness could wait – I had to get somewhere first.

As a BBC journalist, I told stories for a living. It allowed privileged access into the lives of extraordinary people. As the years rolled on and the stories rolled out, I felt increasingly detached from the world I was hired to observe. Like a gawping goldfish inside a bowl, I would compare my own life to others, always wondering – what was remarkable about my own?

Aware of the restlessness gnawing at me, my solution was to take three career breaks to pursue my passion for climbing mountains. However, once I returned to my office routine, it was only a matter of months before that familiar feeling of unrest would set in. The glow of my physical achievements did not last. The changes I had experienced were external and fleeting – only a more decisive change could break an inner deadlock.

I decided to quit my BBC career to immerse in an outdoor life. That was the answer: chasing the seasons across hemispheres, summiting peaks and then finding casual work to fund the next challenge. After eight months of moving from one high-altitude region to another, my dream crashed: I was not only physically burnt out, but had developed a fear of heights. Vertigo was an inseparable part of my climbing experience. An exhausting epiphany dawned: I had substituted the values of my office life at sea level to the snowy heights. One was a lot more comfortable than the other – but neither had yielded fulfilment or the illusive inner peace I craved. There were always more peaks to scale and challenging routes to tackle. No matter how my circumstances changed or wardrobe was weatherproofed, there was never a finishing line when the effort and struggle stopped.

I had an insatiable drive for more. Restlessness was like a twinge, lurking and persistent. As long as I was busy, I could ignore the tension my body was holding. When I stopped or slowed, it started up again. Even my spiritual practices could not quell my discontent. Just like climbing mountains, my experiences only provided short-lived breakthroughs before an urgency arose to get somewhere – anywhere but where I was.

Fed up with the prevailing theme of discontent, which no

manner of new projects could shift, I decided to live a new story. How could I be at peace in this moment, right now, whoever I was or wasn't being, and however things looked or felt? What would happen if I gave up the investment in outcome that kept me living for the future?

The Upside Down Mountain tells that story – from shifting my heady sights upwards, to my descent into the here and now; the immediacy of physical experience in all its sensuous intelligence. Guided by the inner compass of feeling, the book is an invitation, as I experience it, to go down into the body, into the melting pot of buried feeling, the very source of dis-ease. It is a story about facing the darkness of the unconscious and how time collapses when one is no longer constrained by the projected linearity of past and future.

If ascent is as much about ideals, projections, hopes and dreams, then the journey downwards, as I have lived it, is about bodily wisdom: the route into a crushing density of feelings I most want to avoid, that cry for attention when distraction stops.

No human being can escape descent. Shock or trauma, grief or illness will plunge us into darkness and chaos at some point, whatever our resistance. But, descent can also be made consciously, through the journey of embodiment. As I mean it, embodiment unites the worlds of up and down – of possibility and actuality, of our evolved and animal natures – through physical experience. Both are integral to wholeness. To live vibrantly and powerfully means it is no longer enough to be cut off from the neck down. Conscious descent is to face the source of discomfort, the denser instinctual nature exiled from our awareness through shame or fear. To descend consciously means choosing to make peace with those parts of ourselves. To avoid such an undertaking, or to 'grin and bear it', can prolong our suffering or make us ill. In descent, heartbreak becomes as much the key to freedom as bliss.

As a popular mythic map, the Hero's Journey, as conceived by

Joseph Campbell, elevates life into adventure – externalising trials as tools for self-growth. The boon of existential challenge is brought back into the everyday world as medicine for its transformation. The progression through life is represented horizontally, as a quest from one known point into the unknown. In contrast, the heroine's version of epic undertaking would be descent: verticality into the full-blooded physicality of being. Such a route leads *down* and *in*, rather than the hero's trajectory of *up* and *out*.

Neither maps are sourced in gender but in a fundamental difference in relating to life or its storytelling. If quests are the hero's language and expansion their gift, then it's the sensuous that guides a heroine's descent or contraction into her feeling nature. The hero navigates a kingdom represented as outside himself, whereas the heroine's palace is accessed through the gateway of her underworld. To be whole, or balanced, or fully self-realised, can never involve dominance of one way over another. There must be an inner marriage of polarities – the internal and external, or feminine and masculine – for freedom to be fully expressed in human form. And that dance, as I'm discovering, is a lifelong commitment.

As we master the story we tell about ourselves and our relationship to the world, so our creativity flourishes. It requires us to celebrate the paradox of our humanity – for all its perfect flaws. As conscious participators in life's unfolding, we can choose to embody our higher, most illumined states, while keeping true to our uniquely human selves, and how we experience reality.

With all the freedom and power of my childhood stories, *The Upside Down Mountain* is written as a timeless map, unbound from traditional chronology. Divided into four parts – South, West, North and East – each set in a unique place, these cardinal points mirror different aspects of my descent. Some played out unconsciously – as life happening to me, a passive recipient. At a more conscious level, I intended to explore with eyes wide open. And at other times, my descent was a co-creative embodiment, inviting life to happen through me. Along the way, you will be encountering guides who help me penetrate the layers of descent. They are guardians of thresholds within the collective psyche, carriers of wisdom who expanded my awareness and illuminated the next step.

Inspired by the spirit of the 'Upside Down Mountain' itself, Mount Bugarach, I invite you to consider life as an unfolding story that shifts in its telling and to join me in a journey – one in which nothing is really as it is shown, its truth revealed through its experience. There is only one rule to its undertaking – the tale of descent is best felt than understood.

Mags MacKean, Bristol 2015

Introduction

Disguised as a twinge, she has an answer for anyone who questions. For the most part she remains silent, hidden in the shadows – crowded out by decoys, dead ends and false doors. She might make herself known, as she did for me, when purpose and progress, mythologized as a stairway to heaven, no longer makes sense. I know her as Grandmother.

Buoyed by a lifetime of conditioning to want more, do more and be more, restlessness was my constant companion. It wasn't until I felt my way into it and listened hard enough to its wisdom that I discovered the nagging call of Grandmother from the hidden depths of my being.

There's nothing exclusive about our connection, no matter how intimate it can seem. Maybe you have felt Grandmother call to you too. Sometimes I feel her as a little wing, unfurling at my shoulder blades like a tickle or as a sudden impulse to sing. Silent stalker, tender and fierce, she has chased me all my life – long, long before I had any idea I was being trailed. Even when she raged as fierce deadly storms, I was not yet awake to her reminder – the reminder that she was waiting to call me back to the place before the beginning of time, when the story of 'me' began – home.

Grandmother has come as a tarantula – charging me in the jungle, among a throng of people. As guardian of the dreamtime, she assumed a plague of spidery crabs. As harbinger of death, she brings new life. With life, she demands death. It is a reciprocal deal, which will be struck with or without my agreement.

My first encounter with Grandmother in a human identity, so unlike her wilder or more abstract guises, came after a long, long journey, located nowhere with a postcode. The murky waters of my daydreams sparkled with an iridescent phosphorous from the pristine depths into which I had to dive. Descending through the dark density of bone-breaking stillness, I found myself in a fathomless ocean, an unending dimension, the deepest to be found on Earth. Inside the apparently solid core, its hollow interior as vibrantly lit and abundant with life as anywhere miles above it, I was submersed deep within a dormant volcano.

I journeyed to Grandmother that first time with the help of a drumbeat. It propelled me down a tunnel, peaty and moist. My heart raced along as I felt myself pressed down deeper into suffocating darkness. A sudden downpour soon drowned out the rhythmic beats of my heart and the drum. My skin became irritated. How I longed to scratch it, rub away the fever burning through me despite the icy stabs of rain. The water overflowed until there was enough to float upon. I relaxed, weightless and adrift. Then, everything changed. The rain stopped and cheery birdsong filled the pale blue skies of an ordinary spring day. Not a cloud in sight.

A rich smell of damp grass drew me into an orchard teeming with rosy apples, a thatched cottage at one end. Grandmother was stooped beneath a tree, gathering apples to bake. Her white hair was in a bun, her dress too plain to recall. At first glance, her hands were strikingly large, but her eyes were the real giveaway – nothing was as it seemed. They did not belong to a fairy godmother, or a wise witch with a heart tender and expansive from eons of enduring the mixed fortunes of a very long life. No, the eyes that captured mine in the blue translucence of sunlit skies hinted of deep space, enveloping me in all the warmth of an Elysian garden, home-baked wholesomeness, a sanctuary of beehives and roses, blossom and robin-red-breasts.

Her eyes grew as I gazed into them, filling with a sinuous carpet of swallows, pulsing along as one winged bird. "You are the fledgling," I heard her say in the unending stillness. "You are the little wing, the songbird who dreams to soar among the giants of the winged species. All my children are birds living for the only reason there can be."

"And what reason is that?" I couldn't help but ask. "All the little birds are here to sing their hearts out and remember their wings."

I felt my heart open, as I watched Grandmother's eyes change again. They were now galaxies, holding the mysteries of the cosmos, radiant with starlight. A comet flashed at speed until it blazed as the raging, transformative power of fire.

"You're wondering if you're making me up! But I ask you to consider, what isn't story? Is something less real for being imagined? I ask you, how can any physical thing hold more credibility than a dream, when everything – every thought, sensation and whim, and awareness of those things itself – arises within the same space – a space without borders, origin or destination, without beginning and end?"

The earth felt as if it was sliding away from under my feet. The hypnotic flow of her words was seeping through me, releasing me from anything solid. Wasn't everything Grandmother saying familiar, an echo of a distant memory?

"And what now?" I asked. "My life is only too real. But I have the strange feeling sometimes I'm not always in it – a spectator, wondering…"

She interrupted, mimicking my earnestness, "You mean wondering what on earth you are doing here?"

In my mind's eye, there was a giddying blur of movement, countless reinventions of the same old me in work and play; holding a microphone, dancing, cooking, passport controls, mountain ranges, a throng of people, of every creed and colour; the beautiful Earth. If time had run out to live its marvels how I would yearn to live more and more! And wasn't that the point – for all the everyday miracles, the countless reasons to be grateful, there was something not at peace – some…

"Make a friend with it," Grandmother's voice shattered my thoughts. "That very suffering, no manner of external love will heal. Your restlessness is your greatest ally, if you allow it to serve you."

"It is?"

"Yes. It is guiding you back to the beginnings of the beginnings – to a whole new you. It is the doorway to a quantum world, the unlimited possibility of the unknown. There is an opportunity, if you're willing to take it, to begin yourself anew, to recreate your life afresh."

"How?"

"Go to Mount Bugarach, the 'Upside Down Mountain'. The place of fire. Of purification. Feel your way downwards into its mystery, its very heart. Let it show its true nature – less of a place than a state of being."

It was couched as an invitation to explore the very source of turmoil I most wanted to avoid – a journey demanding courage and determination to go beyond anywhere ever imagined and beheld. I was warned that to become identified with any feelings would ensure a hellish experience in the descent ahead. To behold my prospects as just a climb up a mountain was no longer a ticket to anywhere. It would only prolong my misery. There was only one place peace could be found, if compass needles could point to it. The destination, she pointed out, was deep within the molten lava fields inside the belly of the not so dormant volcano.

"Bugarach," she said again, with the faintest trace of a wink. "Don't get too drawn to its form. Like the bullseye, hold it within your sights as a blur, for a greater chance of making your mark. Then feel your way into its depths."

Where I had to go was not only to be reached, she trilled in playful understatement. It was to be brought back, on the great return, as a living memory. It had to merge with all other places held in time, as the remembered arrival it had become. This would be like a slow awakening from the deepest sleep. It was, she told me, the only medicine to soothe the thrum of the most persistent headache.

"You are going to Bugarach – beyond all that has ever been and will be. No one can take you there. It is a journey to be undertaken alone. This is your time to reinvent the story of who you are and have always known yourself to be."

Part I

South – Gateway of Fire

Chapter 1

Meeting Mount Bugarach

After months of dreaming, days in the planning, my arrival at Mount Bugarach coincided with departing high pressure. The sunny morning had begun clouding over as the mountain loomed in the windscreen. Its striking faces rose from dense greenery in every direction, flattening into a gentle slope to the top. Hurtling through the valley, there had been a few false starts: expecting it to appear after each sharp bend. "There she is!" Garth had declared, aware of my excitement. I clapped my hands.

A flurry of cars revved out of the muddy overflow at its base, as my friend swerved on to a bank of grass for an easy exit. A dark belt of cloud was inching closer – not the enticing blue skies of a 'meant to be' rendezvous with Bugarach I had so clearly imagined. Opening the door, I hesitated before straddling over a puddle to join Garth. Lean and tall, he had looked dwarfed squinting up at the well-worn route. He was chewing his glasses which made him sound as earnest as I was beginning to feel. "It's impossible to get lost. But it is going to rain. A bit. Just stick to the path and you'll be fine." I hauled my kit out of the boot and made sure my waterproof gear was at the top. "There'll be a place to pitch up near the summit," he added. "You can't see the flat bit I mean from here. Lots of room there."

"Allow at least one hour 'til then, you said?"

"Possibly two with that weight."

It took some effort to balance the pack, to close the clasp at my hips. It lightened it a little – but it was still heavy, and I was out of practice with hiking under load. I only had the basics: gear for sleeping, two more warm layers and waterproofs, and seven bottles of water. Fourteen litres to last me four days meant fourteen extra kilos to carry. There was no accessible source where I was going. This trip was my version of the Native American rite of passage, a Vision Quest. Traditionally, the solitary immersion in nature equipped boys with life-changing insights and perspectives to be integrated back home as they returned young men. Increasingly the practice bridged into the complex lives of Westerners of any age or sex: or burnt-out professionals like myself needing time out. I too was seeking inspiration. My life needed a kick-start, a fresh direction. Fasting, I knew, was powerful medicine. Going without water, as the original rite held, was too extreme for me. And so the burden of carrying water was unavoidable. Every drop was unlikely to be forgotten in the trudge, clamber and scramble ahead.

I struggled to think of something to keep Garth with me a little longer. Another question eked out our goodbye, about the six-hour long journey he was facing to northern France. He had well-paid work crafting a metal staircase which would fund weeks of rustic living. A blacksmith and artist, Garth had created a simple belle vie in a village not far from Bugarach. A school friend had introduced us via email and he'd put me up – lucky to coincide with his last night at home. Even then, at the outset of my venture, I hankered for one more evening of fun, of good chat and laughter, helped along by Garth's dry humour, the bottle of wine and tasty fare, most of which he'd grown himself. It really was time to get going, Garth said finally, adding he wished he could come too – nothing like reviving in a blast of nature! Next time? He reminded me of the large iron key between two loose bricks beside the front door to his barn. I thought wistfully of his cat Tigger prowling and leaping between high beams, a stray that had arrived one rain-soaked night and never left. Remembering my faded frayed waterproofs, I brushed aside the prospect of long wet hours ahead. It hadn't occurred to me to plan for weather more like winter than spring. "You could make day trips to Bugarach from the barn instead. Nothing wrong with that – I won't think anything less of you!" he smiled. I knew he really meant it. And my grateful refusal, in that moment of goodbye, had been just as sincere. Still, I felt a stab of uncertainty as I set off, wondering how long it might take to find a suitable campsite before heading on to the summit.

I was yearning to experience the unruly space outside the hedgerows of my everyday world – yet grim unease settled over me along the first gentle rise. Tonnes of mud churned by hiking boots and damp looked poised to slide, a viscous river of earth and stone. The path twisted through darkening tree line. Storm clouds gusted closer, lashing drizzle until my face stung. The upper mountain was swallowed whole, greyed as the verdant valleys. I lurched on up the squelching slope, gingerly edging along crustier, less slippery banks. Branches scraped against me and showered more water. A dull ache deep in my stomach was dread for the loneliness of my endeavour, and every other trial surely lying in wait. I paused to get breath.

The landscape looked agitated in the gusts of wind. Ripples of wind-whipped meadow could have been a churning lime-green sea. Not for much longer. Swirling fog was drifting over, limiting visibility in some places to a few metres. My intention to explore the famed corner of the east Pyrenees was losing any romance. It was often said Mount Bugarach was no ordinary mountain. The high-energy magnetism of its limestone hulk had drawn many over the ages. It was a day tripper's ideal: accessible and remote. To my fresh senses, it was unfriendly and something else still – disconcertingly otherworldly. There was no one with whom to moan or commiserate. I had chosen to face this discomfort alone. My eagerness for a quest was growing limper by the moment. The key to Garth's barn flashed in my memory, a vivid taunt. With a sinking feeling, I moved on, overloaded and doubtful.

A glimmer of trail opened up ahead. Rock walls glistened in one direction, charcoal fortresses in my need to find shelter; steep forest the other. Even wild flowers blooming improbably among boulders and silt made the grey flat light more gloomy and hostile. Everything was thwarting my efforts upwards. I stopped again. Shivering, my hands were too numb to release the waist buckle of my sodden backpack. It had become a dead weight. Barely three hundred metres above sea level, it was hard to believe it was late May! The wind was tearing through my dripping gear. Being higher, there was little lee. Bugarach flattened like a field before the last scramble to the summit, as Garth had said. I had little choice but to press on: dash to the top and scout out a campsite before the weather worsened. There had been nothing lower down that would qualify as a last resort: soggy meadows, dense woodland, and steep slope.

I wrestled again with the buckle, eager for another warming layer. Mountains could alter in an eye-blink, but adapting as a fresh-faced visitor to their sudden transformation took longer. Time dragged in struggle. The start of a trip always required transition. My urban skin had to shed so that I could attune to the land's subtle intelligence. Gradually, I would become sensitive to sounds, movements and features, otherwise unnoticeable. So far there had been no such gentle exchange with Bugarach. I was being bludgeoned by its force; repelling my every plodding step, each one already a labour of will; nothing to distract me from the hammering cold and wet.

After one last yank, the backpack dropped to the ground. Only then I realised just how drenched I was, my jacket apparently porous. It had been brand new when I crossed the whole range just south, some eight years before. It had weathered the seventy-two day adventure, skirting the borders of France and Spain. It had also summited peaks in Alaska, the Pacific Northwest, Argentina, Peru, Europe, New Zealand and India. In recent years, it had barely had an outing, wedged at the back of an airing cupboard. It hadn't occurred to me to check over it before heading out to South East France. Not for the first time, I was struck by my blind faith that everything would work out.

My jacket and trousers, made of breathable fabric, allowing a dry exchange of sweat and air, were almost as wet inside as out. Unless the weather cleared dramatically, there would be no chance to get dry.

How the wisdom of Commander Goldsmith an old history teacher was again being vindicated – who branded me in one school report, "an over-enthusiastic butterfly". I had been eight. As my colourful CV since testified, I quickly tired of routine. My life continually felt like an exhausting chase of distractions. An unedited version would have to read: actress, courgette picker, broadcast journalist, traveller, kitchen hand, mountaineer, Amazonian shamanic apprentice, author, coach, energy healer, teacher and speaker. Multiple reinventions of the same old me. Chasing new experiences had become something of a vocation – since quitting my stable life as a BBC journalist, with all its fun, privileged access to people and places, the variety and well-paid rewards – my sea-level life, with its office dynamics and rungs to climb. I had wanted a different sort of ascension – one with the wind in my face, where my hands did real work and my limbs ached. Mountains promised that: endeavour stripped to the quest of a summit and safe descent back into civilised life. And so I climbed, scrambled and roamed, did odd jobs along the way – wherever the whim drove me, until my new outward-bound routine had become as repetitive and exhausting as the one I had escaped from. The values of work or leisure were the same.

After dozens of high altitude trials, it was a relief to grasp I could live just as adventurously in dense concrete jungles – a short drive from the sea. I had virtually given up my mountaineering passion, determined to direct my energy inward – after all, I had reasoned, fed up with my nomadic lifestyle, wasn't life one great big mountain? So I embarked on a whole other journey, from silent retreats in the Himalayas, to the Amazon and its shamanic arts. After nine months of exploring the fear-filled realms within my busy mind, it was clear such efforts were clawing away at the very peace I sought. What was the answer now? The lonely freedom of having enough time and money to make self-driven choices could be just as dispiriting as the commute to work. I felt untethered with or without direction and its accountability. Until hearing of Mount Bugarach and my compulsion to visit it at Grandmother's prompt.

I opened my backpack. Inside were two more tops for warmth. Bedding. A torch. Penknife. A book and notepad. The water. At the very bottom, keeping true to the austerity fitting for a quest, was the lightest tent on the market – then a dubious credential in the stormy circumstances. Keen to lighten the load, I gulped some water back, surprised at my thirst. I looked at my watch. Less than two hours had passed since trudging off, in what had felt like hours of masochistic endurance. My natural optimism was overshadowed by a pragmatic assessment of my options. I was reluctant to leave my pack, in case I found a good spot for the night higher up and had to scamper down and retrace my steps. Given how time was slipping by, I would have to make do with whatever I found.

The wind was getting stronger, unhindered by the valley's undulations. The upper mountain revealed itself before disappearing again. Dramatic serrations pierced the greyness, covered in green-blue mosaics of lichen thriving on the damp rocky spires. Mountain flowers, including mauve orchid and bursts of wild pinks, blues, yellows and whites, peeped between rocks resembling primitive faces. Ghostly faint voices carried in the wind, impossible to locate above or below. I pictured life slowing down far below in the valley. Venturing out was bound to be limited to essential travel and business. I was only feet away from cliffs and sheer falls. There was never room for complacency on a mountain, however small. I'd had many lucky breaks and chances over the years – learning how any minor error such as a slip in footing or navigation could be deadly. A crow cawed, shrill and throaty, startling me from its hidden perch. Its urgency sounded like impatience, a cue to get me moving.

Further along, the grassy plateau Garth had suggested for a campsite was too exposed. There was just enough space to pitch among clumps of gorse, affording reasonable shelter. On closer inspection, a sorry effort had been made to hide toilet roll, with soggy balls of the stuff wedged among rocks. Suitable options for the night ahead were running out. The trail snaked along rocky slabs to the summit. A flattish spot had been cleared of rocks as a rudimentary windshield, with off-putting bits of torn carton, a beer can and orange peel worn into the dirt. It was also right next to the path, too public to feel secure. Surely wild camping, I thought despairingly, meant a place without a human trace.

As I gained height, it was all too clear there was nowhere flat or sheltered enough to camp. I wondered whether Bugarach would seem as impenetrable if the sun was shining. In the build-up to coming, I'd imagined a gentle interplay with the mountain – paying homage after responding to its call. Nothing could have seemed less likely. I had yet to find my footing there. Perhaps this was why it was known as 'the Upside Down Mountain'. Bugarach had its oldest rock at the top and youngest underneath – inspiring one theory that it flipped over from the impact of a meteorite. Or perhaps tectonic forces ruptured the Earth's crust to form the mountain, as layers of geology reshuffled, pushing the oldest to the top of the pack. In any event, the area was charged with undisputed natural power. Such was its electromagnetism, compasses could be wildly affected, causing havoc with navigation. Whatever lay ahead on that rain-blasted mountain, the experience was bound to reset my inner compass.

Already I had a sense of the unyielding mystery of Bugarach. Its distinctive flavour couldn't be compared to anywhere else. My tension hadn't let up for one moment. It felt like I was facing an initiation of sorts into the famed mountain's many aspects. It drew a spectrum of enthusiasts: the rambler, geologist, climber, caver, seeker, pilgrim, healer, romantic, UFO spotter, Magdalene worshipper, Cathar, conspiracy theorist, Ark of the Covenant quester, birdwatcher and botanist. From the moment I first read about Mount Bugarach, my imagination was captured: a mountain of distinctive geology and human appeal was going to have seams of hidden stories to be unearthed!

Until the Victorians, only an eye-blink ago in time's scale, the heights were believed to house creatures of darkness, such as dragons and otherworldly beings. They were places of haunt and exile, as well as celestial promise. Those more daring pioneers who took off to explore them were branded hero or fool, the mountain as much a gateway to hell's inferno as heaven's peace. Lust, envy, hate and the rest were said to scream in the purification of extreme heat. For a sinner or seeker, drawn to fire or height, the mountain meant transformation. Any opening into the Earth, however large or small, was a gateway to realms beyond death. And, I reminded myself, my feet were plodding over a mountain famed for its passages and caves, doorways to stories outside the everyday. Bugarach's apparent solidity, to swallow the bravado of legend, was anything but. No wonder it had been a documented place of pilgrimage for centuries, for adventurers into the unknown. And for me.

Rounding the final twist to the top, I was almost knocked flat. The tapping of hiking sticks was carried by the wind, before an elderly couple in woolly hats and with altimeters strapped to well-proofed jackets bounded down from the hidden summit. They looked as if they'd hiked all over the world in a long marriage, with strong bronzed faces, walking steadily without showing any surprise at seeing me.

"Le pic est la bas, juste la?" I asked for the sake of it, gesturing to the only possible summit point.

"Oui, continuez, juste la… deux minutes encore… attention du vent!"

Such exchanges were comforting in unlikely places, for all their ordinariness. I dumped the pack, mindful of the cliffs the other side of a second path descending a steeper route. A hump of rocks signalled the highest point. I touched it as a point of pilgrimage. As if in answer, the wind gusted at a force I could lean into with nearly all my weight. With nothing to see, everything white, and my body supported, I could almost forget I had one. Opening my arms wide, like a bird, I felt airborne. Without putting up some resistance, the wind could have blown me clean off. The exposure was liberating, and wildness unchecked. There was no responsibility to anyone or anything except myself – flying on the peak of Bugarach!

Closing my eyes, I pictured the land hundreds of feet below, perforated with limestone caves and passages. "Whatever it is I'm really seeking," I thought, "may I be open to discovery, and accept all that comes my way... always in my highest good," I tagged on. Just in case. For life had always given me whatever I'd asked, even when I hadn't knowingly asked.

I raced down to retrieve my gear, enjoying my levity and ease leaping between rocks. Back on the plateau, I ruled out staying there, after another thorough search for a site. Beyond it on steeper ground was an intriguing formation of rock. It made me think of a cave, the best possibility for dry rest. Only a slope of dense shrub requiring some crawling to get through separated me from perfect shelter – of that I was certain! Once again, I dropped the weight and twisted and crouched my way through the prickly undergrowth. I puffed up a narrow gully of scree, continually snarled by thorns. A sheer wall of rock became a handrail, shielding me from thin air the other side. I'd heard of hermits throughout the ages living in caves in Bugarach and half-expected some bearded robed ghost to materialise.

After exhausting effort, I reached a flat area where the scree levelled off. There was no cave as I had imagined, only a nook between rocks, with a sheer drop one side. They were still high enough to nestle against and shield me from the wind and some rain. The spot was hidden too; an advantage from straying hikers.

My positivity soon wore away during the arduous scramble back to my pack. Going down took as much persistence as going up. I couldn't face that again. Given my fast ahead and how wet I already was, it would be a struggle to keep warm. I had to preserve my physical energy. It was only a matter of time, of holding out, I reasoned: there was the perfect campsite waiting to be discovered lower down. It had simply eluded me on the way up.

The path widened at the tree line, still too steep to camp. The fog clouds had turned the woods into a moist fairyland of moss, bracken, toadstools, guarded by giant boulders. I felt watched, imagining elves and goblins peering out from behind trees and hidden burrows. The path wound on, reaching the fields approaching the lower slopes. The decision of where to stay my first night was decided. There was nowhere else but the mud nearing the car park, or the other side of a fence, where the grass was long and land flat enough to guarantee soggy conditions. I scouted out the driest surface among some pine trees.

It was a challenge unearthing my camping gear from plastic liners without getting everything else wet. I regretted packing my down sleeping bag – warmer and lighter than a synthetic one, but impossible to keep dry. The tent pitched, it took an age fumbling about getting everything organised inside. Everything felt damp – my spares, my bedding – and I hadn't even spent a full day on the mountain. The low front wasn't going to lift any time soon. There was no chance of drying out during the rest of my time on Bugarach.

I unravelled my mat and sleeping bag and tucked myself up. A choice of two sorry apples, the sole prospect of food before the fast began, preoccupied me next. Which one first – red or less red? A small puddle had gathered at my bent elbow. Water was seeping in from underneath. I sighed, too tired to swear, too despondent for any reaction more dynamic. Only an unanswerable question: What am I doing here?

My voices of rash and reason began to battle it out: well, this was the plan, and it was on track! If everyone on a vision quest gave up at the first sign of challenge, the rite of passage would never have outlasted thousands of years of evolutionary culture. The effort of optimism was too tiring. The train of a small spider roaming the damp floor reminded me of my own solitary vulnerability. What am I doing? Yes, what was I doing? I had no reason to choose such discomfort, and no motivation to prolong it – for it had been a long road since I left my London life, pension, Notting Hill flat and thriving network. "It was a new life, a fresh start, a dream," I had explained rather smugly to those who labelled me brave. Well, it had taken a little longer and many social collisions later to work out lasting change could not be external. You could tweak the environment, climb some mountains, try out a new boyfriend, live in a new home, forsake the office life. You could move to the Amazon, train with shamans, reinvent yourself ad infinitum, flirt with different continents, places and people, never quite taking the plunge to commit to life as it is right now – every decision invested with a sense of tomorrow. You could set yourself up as the world's most inspired motivator or coach or change consultant – after all, a life committed to change, such as mine, knocked up some first-hand authority; publish a book, write some more, speak about it, meet audiences just as inspired to escape their life, and then meet some more. The airport could trigger the same rush as getting high – the ticket to a new horizon, the thrill of adventure, possibility, endless new influences. The merry-go-round of seasonal themes, the cycles, patterns, and déjà vu moments, the doomed love, broken dream, the mended, hopeful, eager heart, the hollow words of arrival, "I'm really sorted now, this is it!" Or false start: "This is my vocation – what I'm born to do!" There was always one common denominator, and that never changed. It followed me, pursued my every move a hungry shadow, no matter how stuffed my suitcase, and how far flung or extreme my destination. For, time and again, being out 'there' and waking up to the only place there had ever been and would be – 'here' – could only mean that no matter how hard I climbed, danced, loved or laughed, cried and celebrated, meditated, quested, retreated, tranquillised, inquired, chanted, fasted and prayed, there really was – and always had been – and (if that was not exhausting enough to accept) there always would be… no-thing but me!

I peered out of the tent and took a deep breath to clear my mind. "Mount Bugarach," I invoked silently. "I'm here to open up to whatever has pulled me to this unlikely place – given I don't know what that is. I'll stay all week if that's what I need to do. But please – help me to know – just give me a sign!"

Almost at once, I sensed a reply.

"The way up is down."

I closed my eyes again, intending verification. It was too easy to imagine what I most wanted to hear.

"To go up, you must go down…"

Clarity was a wonderful thing: when you knew you knew, and until you knew, you didn't know. Suffering and sacrifice, which I had tasted, were not apparently a requisite to path finding or way-showing. A quest with the prospect of bed, dry, hot food – why not? I had to trust there was another design, another way…

Within minutes, the soaked tent was stuffed into my pack. I would have to relay my gear, not having the energy or will to reorganise everything to fit in as it did dry. Already 7pm. I smiled, remembering Bugarach's 'Upside Down' nickname. The way up was down. Stomping back towards the valley, I relished my retreat to civilisation, wishing I could share the unlikely twist with Garth, who would surely be imagining me hunkered down with spirited discipline. Having explored with dogged persistence a life moving uphill, who was I not to investigate, consciously, the opposite direction? What did 'down' mean anyway that I hadn't before experienced – and where could it

Chapter 2

Time of the New Age

The next morning, between downpours, I had dashed to the one café open for business in Bugarach village. A weather report taped to its door was a blur of low-pressure squiggles and black drops. No change for the next few days: remaining cold, windy and wet until after my departure. I headed for a table closest to a glowing stove in view of a woman heaping fresh produce on to platters for the delicatessen. Combs of honey, chopped herbs, cured meats and cheeses, simple and elegant, made me hanker for an early lunch. Customers streamed in, muttering disbelief as they shook off wet coats, conversations springing up as the windows steamed. The place had become a hub in the cheerlessness, time slowing to a soothing din of chatter, an espresso maker's throttled blasts and doorbell as someone came and went. Panpipes whistled from a speaker, sweet tinkles of the Andes in the foothills of France.

A nearby window framed an ongoing drama, with all its tension: would the sun triumph through thinning fog? Intermittent fringes of light, small rainbow spheres, boded well – until it darkened again and the manageress turned on more lights. Still, weather was a local peculiarity, varying from one valley to the next: perhaps my fast was only a temporary postponement, the mountain reappearing. My spirits lifted at the prospect of stepping foot on it again, until I remembered the mud bath around its base, no doubt thicker and more glutinous after another night and morning of rain. The prospect of finding a way through it arrested further skips of faith. I had ended up in the only place with beds open for business: an empty gîte overlooking its western flank. From the shelter of its porch, tantalising glimpses of the mountain's silhouette had come and gone. That was what I had to settle for of Mount Bugarach, touched up with some imagination. My patience was being tested. The mountain had clearly told me to go down: but did not say for how long. Surely I was not going to eat and sleep my way through the remaining days of this quest?

Voices trailed into the tussle of my hopes and disappointment. A man was recounting how the wind had made it impossible to summit Bugarach the day before. Sweeping gestures conveying its full force suggested a cyclone had engulfed Bugarach. Too dangerous – a suicide mission. Silence followed, which I felt compelled to interrupt – for there had been a few of us at the top – but for sure, I conceded, it had been hard work in that weight of wind. "Non, impossible! C'est le summit ce que je dige," the man answered.

I had meant the summit, Monsieur. There was only one. It was true the wind was very strong. Still, it had been possible. "Impossible, Madame," he replied, more uncertainly that time, addressing the floor. Resuming, his voice was conciliatory, "Alors, voila! Vous avez la chance!"

If it had been luck, as he had said, enabling me to sample the mountain's unforgiving power, then I yearned for more of it. I ordered another coffee. A cyclist in soaked Lycra strode in and huddled next to the stove. It was getting mustier with all the towels and jackets drying out over seats. The manageress was busying herself about a reclining chair draped in blankets. A woman promptly installed herself on it and stretched out. A hum started up as the chair vibrated and woman wobbled. Catching my eye, the manageress explained as she breezed past, "Crystals underneath. She's being charged." I could see her client was well prepared for whatever the bed was there to do. Already she had put on a blindfold, her mouth as wide open as someone passed out.

This was Bugarach – not just any postcard mountain village. When I had arrived bedraggled at the gîte the night before, the owner had told me it was indeed a special place drawing special people. It wasn't always easy to live there either. There was a continual tension, she told me, an electromagnetism intensifying daily ups and downs. Until the age of satellite, even light aircraft were banned from within a certain radius to avoid disorientation in a mini Bermuda Triangle.

Although the region was rich in history with many ruined hilltop castles and trails of knights, battles, invading armies and religious sites, most who came to Bugarach village had the famed peak within their sights. All around it, abundant verdure sprung from underground grottos and passageways natural to limestone. Such labyrinths courted adventure as well as exploration of a more passive kind: speculation of parallel worlds and otherworldly beings inside them. It was rumoured there were caves waiting to be discovered – housing evidence of suppressed human history. Our anthropological lineage would be rewritten in such event, and the vested interest of those hiding the 'real' story of our evolution exposed.

A high-energy place was bound to inspire conjecture among more creative thinkers. I wasn't at Bugarach to flirt with a radical view of the world – although its background of sensational claims certainly added spice to my venture. I wanted to forge a connection uniquely my own. But glancing over my notes, the bullet points seemed as random and fantastical as the rumoured conspiracies I dismissed. There were bare bones of leads to chase, as well as unsubstantiated material gleaned from the Internet.

"2012. Bugarach – link to Egypt. Eclipse – potential for what? Modern link? ... Essenes and Magdalene? Chalice mystery... Glastonbury/Avalon. My link to these?"

An unanswerable question threaded through all the others – would they weave together in my emerging story at Bugarach? Anything was possible. It was 2012 after all, the hyped date of Armageddon imprinted in the popular psyche. The area's mystique was heightened among those who laid stock on the approaching Winter Solstice, and even those who didn't. The interpretation of its foretold significance varied in outcome but not in impact: mass destruction for the planet at one end, or the death of outworn values and birth of a love-centred new era at the other. Ancient sites all over the world were seeing more visitors, as well as places charged in natural power, like Mount Bugarach.

Dreamers, seekers and new age prophesy followers had begun to besiege the village in recent years. There were increasing accounts of unexplainable lights emanating from the mountain. Theories to explain those and other strange sightings covered a spectrum of plausibility: from natural electromagnetic activity typical of its geology, to UFO landings and even alien beings waiting to live out the days of imminent apocalypse. Wherever one sided in relation to such hypotheses, sceptic or believer, popular curiosity about Bugarach wasn't new. There was something about the 'Upside Down Mountain' or 'Magic Mountain' as it was also known which had spawned legends throughout the ages – and somehow it had taken life within my own imagination as a muse of some kind for my own personal journey.

I thought about a bigger human story that threaded through epochs, cultures and continents – the tug of home and land. Pilgrims had crossed continents since ancient times, tracking a sacred chemistry uniting such sites. There was a universal lineage I could sense at places of power, such as Mount Bugarach – where the beliefs and myths of our ancestors to explain the world could be most keenly felt. At the time of Roman rule, a thriving Essene community had settled at Bugarach. They had emigrated from the Promised Land, possibly via Mount Sinai in Egypt, whose temples along the Nile would have offered rites and initiations. Some Essenes were known to have moved on to Britain's Druid centres of the Isle of Anglesey, or Mona as it was known, and

Glastonbury, or Avalon, and Iona, the Emerald Isle, off Scotland's western coast. Those same places on the Essenes' trail lived vividly in my memory – Egypt in particular, having made three visits in one year to soak up its unending archaeological magic. So Bugarach, as far as its documented history suggested, was linked to Egypt and Glastonbury – two places that had most inspired in me a sense of the sacred.

Other histories woven into the mountain's fame required more faith: Jesus spending time there with his fellow Essenes as he journeyed on to Albion's shores; Mary Magdalene living out her time in one of the region's caves. The famous chapel of Rennes-le-Château nearby was dedicated to her and her legendary healing powers with water from the area's springs. Long after the invading Roman armies at the time of Jesus' life, and suppression of pagan custom, the Cathars then had a part in the Languedoc region's romance. The Puritan peace-loving Christian sect was feared by the dominant Catholic hierarchy for their empowering teachings. Hounded by the French Inquisition, they were brutally killed in large numbers for heresy: refusing to believe in the Church's dogma, or worship their icons such as a cross. The Knights Templar blazed through the area on their quest for the grail. The ubiquitous ruined ramparts also spoke of powerful kingdoms and territories, rocky buttresses impenetrable to the invading armies of the Middle Ages. Secret societies were known to have spent time in the area, further romanticising legends of the Divine Feminine and her mysteries to be reclaimed. The Ark of the Covenant, carrying the Ten Commandments, was again linked to Mount Bugarach. Conspiracy theories argued the likelihood of it being hidden within the mountain's secret heart. Intriguing graffiti showing a stretcher bearing a chest, found etched on to cave walls, intensified the intrigue.

The discovery was made by 'Daniel Bettex', the one name scribbled among my notes. For more than thirty years, the Swiss explorer researched the Cathars' connection to the mountain and its caves. In 1997, on the eve of his last trip to the area, Bettex claimed to be within three days of making the ultimate discovery – the mystery of the Ark of the Covenant's whereabouts. No further word was ever heard from him again. His body was found without a clear cause of death. Was it a heart attack, or had he died of shock? His sudden and unexplained death fuelled speculation about Bugarach's hidden history. Even before Bettex's well-documented fascinations, the Nazis of the Third Reich were thought to have bored tunnels into the mountain. Whatever for? Even François Mitterrand's helicopter had once landed on the flat plateau close to the summit. Why? The French President had been recovering from heart surgery. Might the mountain's known vibrations and energy have been sought for healing? No one knew.

I too was caught up in Bugarach's metamorphosis from mystic mountain to popular attraction. The pessimistic forward planning of its Mayor had inspired world headlines – after alerting the army to protect his village from a deluge of visitors and suicide cults, in the countdown to the Winter Solstice six months on of 2012. There was a cross-cultural consensus of many traditional cultures foretelling an evolutionary leap for humanity – to extend far beyond the suggested impact of one specific day, December 21st 2012. The Maya, Zulu, Maori, Aborigine, Kogi, Zuni, Navaho, Hopi, Kahuna and Qu'ero were among the tribes to share with the world similar ancient wisdoms. For thousands of years an auspicious alignment of stars was forecast for the Winter Solstice of the Northern Hemisphere: the Earth positioned directly beneath the heart of the Milky Way, known as the 'Great Cleft' or 'Rift'. For the ancients this symbolised a deeply feminine aspect, also called the Great Mother. The times were foreseen as an opportunity to transform our awareness as a species about our inseparability from the whole cosmos; we would awaken to the unity of nature and our inherent divinity as loving caretakers of all life. Over time, our wounds would heal as a collective, transforming our relationship to our feminine nature and Mother Nature herself. By rebalancing our values, we would remember the good of the whole over the senseless promotion of the self. War, destruction, harm to others and greed could no longer be the fallout of an overzealous patriarchal order.

As the prophesies foretold and leading visionaries agreed, it was a time for human beings everywhere to marry the feminine and masculine expressions of life within themselves, not indulge one over the other. The upheaval of governing structures and economies around the world fed into the credibility of the prophesies. 'Empowerment' was the language of change, the shift from outside authority to self-determination, and owning one's inner mastery. In the West, NGOs, volunteer and community interest groups were flourishing, courses for healing and self-inquiry no longer a minority interest. There was a revival of interest in the earth-based spirituality of our ancestors. Their values of reciprocity inherent to indigenous cultures chimed with many discontented with capitalism.

There was no evidence around Bugarach I had seen of a mass refuge from planetary wipeout. Few I had encountered looked on the wackier end of spiritual curiosity. The tourism of early summer was still some weeks away and Bugarach that May was an ordinary sleepy Pyrenean village. I looked away from my notes, the fug from the stove making me drowsy. Right then, I should have been somewhere on the mountain, sipping water, on the first morning of my fast. I felt no regret – only a curiosity for what lay ahead now my plans had surrendered to Mount Bugarach's instruction, as I had understood it, to descend. I had no impulse to do anything or go anywhere – only a dwindling optimism that I'd somehow stumble across the deeper purpose of my visit.

Another stranger wandered into the café and looked about for somewhere to sit. He asked if he could share my table then began talking to a woman with '2012' in large garish font on the front cover of her book. The man had a thick accent – hard to place – and spoke limited French. The 2012 prophesies, they exchanged, were interesting – very much so. Now was the time for a change in consciousness – people were waking up everywhere. Bugarach, he said, was an important centre for this change. True, she agreed. After enthusing about her book, spelling out the author's surname so he could make a note of it, she wished everyone in the room a good day and left. Acknowledging my neighbour, I exclaimed in French that Bugarach was surprisingly empty of visitors.

"Yes. But wait – in December, the solstice, it will be different." I nodded at him, and swigged some more coffee. "I'm Patrick, by the way," he added in more confident English. "... And you are – ?"

"Mags. Nice to meet you." I only noticed then how dishevelled he seemed in a thin, worn jacket, unsuited for rugged weather. Mine looked the part but was perhaps as useless as his. His small bloodshot eyes peered out of a tangled mop of hair, looking rough and sweet at the same time. We were the same age I guessed, and yet his worn lined face suggested he'd lived the harder.

He nodded at my notes. "Do you mind if I ask you what you're writing?"

"Oh, just scribbling some things – observations about the Bugarach area and what to find out about while I'm here. They don't make a lot of sense, but help me piece stuff together when I get back home. My version of a diary."

"Mmm. I have this," he said, slipping his hand into a bag to place several lenses on to the table beside an impressive camera.

"This is my memory stick!"

"Oh really? Are you passing through taking photos?"

"That depends. I'm here to... document stuff, you know? This mountain Bugarach is pretty crazy and there's some wild stuff going on here!" He pronounced Bugarach with a softened French ending. I preferred the edge of its more guttural English name. We both sipped our coffees, not in any rush to fill the silence. Patrick looked as if he hadn't slept in days, pale and twitchy from caffeine. His eyes roamed the room, as if hunting for something to speak about.

"This is a crazy place. That's why I'm here," he declared out of the blue. Portuguese and living in London – he was, please don't judge, a paparazzi. That jolted me back to my old life as a reporter – mingling with the paparazzi throngs outside courts and high-profile events, often more entertaining than the story we had been sent to cover. Their frenzy for the perfect shot to earn a crust often turned into aggressive jostle, a media crowd wheezing and crammed against security barriers. There were so many variables to capturing a story in a picture, and nothing could be left to chance for an editor to buy it. Patrick had an edge – but didn't have that hungry look, the tough skin, to survive such a gritty profession. As if reading my thoughts, he explained how times were even tougher, so he was scouting out his own scoop at Bugarach. He had hitched there the day before, and like me, unprepared for the hostile weather. Our rapport was sealed: both laughing at our obvious misfortune. He was following the heads-up of those he encountered to meet others with their own story to tell, their own take, such as the Mayor of Bugarach. "Yeah, I hope to see him tomorrow. He has been... let us say, doing quite well out of this whole 'Upside Down Mountain' story. It's crazy, you know, there's money in this! There are some people who are selling rocks from this place on the Internet... no joke! You order per kilo. The energy here is being sold. It's all so – "

"Crazy?" I suggested.

"Crazy!" he agreed.

"I read somewhere the Mayor was trying to keep the busloads of New Agers away from here. You can hardly blame him."

"Well, I hope to know more tomorrow. I keep leaving messages. No answer."

"And I wanted to camp on Bugarach – no such chance!"

"So, what about you – why are you here?" he asked, eyeing me steadily.

"It seemed a good place to work out what to do with my life... but I may have to find something else to do!" I shrugged, turning to the window. "We're both here searching for a story – funny who you end up meeting!"

We caught eyes, both of us smiling at our common ground. Patrick was seeking the story of other people. I wanted to discover my own. For all our apparent differences, we shared the same weary faith that in showing up at the foot of Mount Bugarach our impulsive arrival would start to make sense. He was lost and so was I.

"You've heard some of those UFO stories?" Patrick asked, quite matter-of-factly.

"No," I answered curtly, not wanting to waste time with more flaky hearsay. Straying into extraterrestrial territory was hardly going to guide me anywhere useful. There was nothing original I could add to Patrick's Bugarach dossier either, who then talked me through a list of appointments set up in nearby Rennes-les-Bains and Rennes-le-Château. I was able to share some observations of the area, having sped along winding back lanes first thing that morning in a hired car – the enchanting mix of fairy tale castles, groves of oak and rocky monoliths towering over the land like sentinels; the goat, sheep and cow roaming the lush hills beneath large cruising hawks, a peaceful contrast to the remains of bloodied history. Rennes-le-Château's cobbled charm and its spacious hilltop setting had been impressive. Despite being a tourist magnet, Mary Magdalene's chapel, with its blue murals and esoteric symbols, had a strong energy. In one window, Magdalene's image – her long auburn locks and blue cloak, alabaster jar, and skull of death beside her – was, to my eyes, an open challenge to the Bible's depictions of her passive presence in Jesus' circle. "Well, I've heard it's a really dark place, you know," Patrick cut in. "Strange rituals go on there... it's like there are those crazy people who use the place to do weird stuff!"

Conspiracy theories made me weary, for all their seductive intrigue; 'what ifs', 'whys' and 'surely' could quickly flare into certainty, hunch becoming rant. Patrick was not engaging with that intensity so far but I was unwilling to find out if he would. Perhaps sensing this, he changed the subject and asked about somewhere to stay. I told him my gîte was clean and empty – a sound, cheap bet. "Maybe I'll see you later," he said, extending his hand.

"Good luck," I replied. "Hope you find some new leads."

I too needed a lead and returned to my notes. Of course – I had forgotten there would be a solar eclipse that night. Although visible only in parts of America and the South Pacific, the timing was synchronous, carrying all the more magic for being unplanned. A friend had also pointed out this eclipse was special – it fell on the same day in May honoured thousands of years before in an important Egyptian rite, marking a mystical union of the feminine and masculine. The bovine Goddess of fertility Hathor came together with her consort Horus, the vulture God with his all-seeing eye, in a perfect harmony of Yin and Yang energies. It was a festival celebrating the worlds of Earth and all above, at their most balanced.

Being at Bugarach on such an anniversary felt auspicious – given vultures were so much a part of the Pyrenean landscape, as well as my longing to return to the sites and temples of Cairo and the Nile. I had been to Egypt three times the year before, inspired by its ancient wonders. To my heart, the standard history of the temples and pyramids was laced up storytelling, to explain their likely function and even age. I preferred the mystery – and all its unanswerable questions. Whatever the truth, the myths, rites and cosmology of Egypt's ancient lore, showing life on Earth as inseparable from the skies, remained beautiful. And, once again, I was being reminded of Bugarach's link to Egypt, recorded in my scribbles.

Despite the weather forcing my descent, that rare convergence seemed like a blessing to my being there at all. This was fresh inspiration indeed to shape the grey blustery day: I would make a small offering beneath the mountain that evening, to mark the eclipse, the new moon – and the generous instruction to go down into the dry warm refuge of the valley. There was a glimmer – faint but unmistakable – of benevolence in the forces frustrating my original plan. All I could do was focus on the next step, trusting that at some point a new direction with all its untapped promise would have to open up at last.

Chapter 3

Invoking Fire

An hour before sundown, I trudged through sodden fields of long damp grass towards a man-made lake outside the village. From there, a path wound on along a river, the other side of the mountain. At a glance it looked even bleaker than where I'd been the day before – not surprising for a remoter and more challenging way up the summit. Wispy trunks of silver birch were glowing in the dimming light, their leaves rustling like whispers. Dusk was a moody time for me, the sunlit world of nature poised to withdraw into the encroaching dark. I felt watched. My approach seemed boisterous, unsettling a dynamic holding together the elements of place – plant, mineral and animal.

Everything was unnaturally still for all the wind, only gently stirring; the trees, bush and long wild grass somehow captured within a frame of time. Even large boulders, churned from the mountain in a glacial sweep, looked arrested mid-fall in their rightful place. There seemed nothing incidental about the cluster they formed in that one spot – and yet I couldn't imagine any reason for human interference. They were like jolly old sentinels who might break into a chat or snigger as soon as my back was turned. I had the urge to see if they would roll with the gentlest prod. My hand on the edge of one, I only felt its unquestionable density. But by tilting my head and narrowing my eyes, every angle, chip and notch in the shifting light seemed to animate, as if these solid stones might spring into life any moment.

There was ceremony in simply showing up beneath the mountain in my drenched boots, alert and present. I wriggled my toes, picturing their wrinkled puffy whiteness squelching in damp socks. The river before me was a foaming torrent, the earth sodden and spit thickening into rain, some drops splattering on my head and hands with an audible pop, icy cold. Everywhere so much water – land being washed over, the spindly track disappearing into swamp, the river racing on in unbreakable fury towards flatter, more open space. It would be dangerous to cross such churning force.

The rain was driving harder, water bleeding from every crack and verge. Nature was never at heart a containable force – its essence was elemental, impersonal – no apology for the life-death dance of human tenants fighting to civilise it. And that's what I took for granted every day – walking along conveniently paved roads, dropping in somewhere for a ready-made bite to eat, the artificial ways to keep me warm and dry. Watching on as the river raged, the idea of damming rivers, boring tunnels, building towering skylines to withstand its tempest unleashed seemed pure hubris. And every day, the bricks and mortar of my house also barricaded me against its bite or caress, the cold, rain, wind and heat; every modern comfort insulating my own wild nature. My cosy life was not just a privilege but an anaesthetic. No wonder chasing happiness was exhausting – it went against the law of nature. It was to set up unending disappointment.

Back towards the gîte, blood-orange clusters of wild poppy were being pounded by wind and rain, so fragile and resilient. The other way, the upper protrusions of Bugarach disappeared again behind swirling mists. Its haunting secrets were taking life around me – the mountain's south flank now peeping through the fog sweeping across the valley. My eye was drawn to a long deep cleft slashed into a wall of rock. Enfolded by creases and serrations, it began to resemble a giant vulva the more I looked on. Such a dramatic feature would have inspired in ancient times a story for being there, I decided; the land's contours voicing the forces of creation for the ancestors. Perhaps an inviting feminine symbol embedded within the impenetrable-looking rock would play a part in my emerging story too – given how struck I was by its oddity.

Just as I thought that, I had a strong intuition for the next day: to approach the mountain from that direction, via the south. South was also, as I had been taught in the Andean tradition, the direction associated with the element fire. Fire ignited the power of dreams; it transformed the old and potentiated the new. The Medicine Wheel encompassed the cardinal points to represent levels of experience – physical, mental, soul and spirit. Life, in the ancient map of consciousness, was a continual circuit of the wheel: its cycles of death, rebirth and everything in between. Journeying from the east, south, west and north held different teachings along the way. To complete a revolution invited a deeper exploration every time it was undertaken. The directions helped chart otherwise unnavigable territories, each one necessary to explore, in the desire to become whole. It made so much sense to me. Working with fire, I knew, meant a rapid return on any intention. The element was like rocket fuel, powering up desires and their manifestation. It was the spirit of assistance necessary to help break through my mental resistance.

First, layers of personal history had to be shed for the new to take life. Cutting ties with the past, and its ghosts, was essential to ease the passage forwards. That's what I had to do: loosen attachments to anything outworn or no longer serving me – like the unconscious fears and thoughts holding me back. It would make sense that a south-facing route coincided with an ancient gateway for inner alchemy and outward manifestation. I imagined how initiates in times past might have started their journey that same way, to harness the power of fire to transform the elements of life into gold. At last, a new direction was opening up; for the first time that day, I felt excited with impetus. There was still a chance, right then I was sure of it, to step beyond a life-changing threshold the mountain guarded.

I reached into my pockets for three stones from places special to me. They were to be given to the river as offerings, tokens of the exchange necessary on my part to receive the gift of the unknown in the days ahead – however that might look. One was from the beach near my childhood home; another from Glastonbury, strikingly shaped like the Tor where I found it; and the third from West Kennet Long Barrow – a megalithic chambered tomb, steeped in ancestral power and perfectly aligned to Silbury Hill, Britain's own pyramid, Stonehenge and the rest of the Avebury temple complex. Each stone had an energy, a palpable physical charge. It wasn't surprising given where they came from. All temples and sacred sites – natural or constructed – had a strong natural electromagnetism in their quartz-rich soil. The worlds of above and below were united in the positioning of stones and altars. Each one was related to the movement of sun and stars, and aligned to the Earth's geomagnetic forces. Like vast calendars, their precision betrayed a sophisticated knowledge of astronomy, maths and philosophy. I relished how some of the world's most celebrated heritage was found on my own ancestral lands, the UK shores once known as 'Albion'. There was not only a web of real physical currents connecting them, but a collective human story I imagined weaving through the stones and land too.

Acknowledging the directions around me, and the hidden mountain nearby, I threw in the first stone – for the ghostly guardians of the land. As soon as it hit the water, there was a flash of understanding – that fire birthed all worlds, all life, giving rise to the new and unborn. Accessing Bugarach its south-facing side, true to my hunch, would help open my heart to its mysterious depths. The next was for all those I loved in my life – for those I knew and those still to meet. Silently, I called on the spirit of courage to allow the old and outworn within me to die. As it sank, I knew the renunciation of what was familiar to me – my everyday thoughts about the world – were a sacred exchange with the spirit of Bugarach. So far I had felt its tough love in urging me to retreat to the warm shelter of the valley. Despite the surprising hostile weather, it had not crossed my mind to head home.

I hurled in the third stone, for the untameable heart of mine. The unruly spirit of nature, so evident around me right then, was longing to be made known and felt in me! I also threw in some wild flowers picked on my way to the river. The yellows and pinks, and their straggly stalks, disappeared in the water's bubbling surface, before snarling up among gathered branches. They then freed up again, drifting away in wide circles.

A lone star peeped out of clouds being blown across the darkening sky. My stones, carried to France, were on a riverbed beneath Mount Bugarach. I had fulfilled my intention to offer them – and received one new impulse for the next day – to head round the wilder side of the mountain's base, and see what might happen next. The quest had taken an unforeseen twist, and with no better ideas, all I could do was respond to every impulse, however small. I was shivering, only now aware of how cold I had become as well as ravenously hungry. It was time for the snug warmth of my room, the radiator set to maximum. Turning towards the village, the draw of its electric comfort inspired me to walk briskly. My legs felt stiff and cold, but quickly loosened as I warmed up. Slowly, lights began to take the form of buildings, with their promise of hot comforting food. A foray to the one restaurant open that evening became more and more enticing, with my every determined stride towards it.

Chapter 4

Meeting the Weaver

There had been a rim of light framing the door opposite mine back at the gîte. It was bound to have been Patrick who'd ended up there, I had decided, fumbling with a key, before stepping into a fetid fug of drying clothes. Being empty of anyone else, the gîte seemed all the more orderly and soulless – glaring strip lights activated by echoing steps beneath them, any hint of life like an upset, every sound and fleck of dirt standing out all the more. As I fell asleep the movements of the stranger became something to listen to – in the passage outside to the bathroom, or door slamming on a zealous weight.

During the night the rain was relentless. It lashed against the window and roof like a drumroll, lulling me into a labyrinth of intensely vivid dreams. Somewhere in that twilight time before first light, there was a dream that was to alter the course of everything still to happen at Mount Bugarach. I met a woman unsettlingly familiar – and everything about our encounter, upon waking up, felt incomplete, as if our chemistry still had to be played out.

The dream began with a hearth, flames rising like fiery spires, cracking and spitting up the cast iron chimney from a glow of coals and kindling. A wooden wheel was spinning beside a small square window, branches frapping against it in a whistling wind. The room seemed low and squat, nestled into the earth to withstand the forces unleashed at it. I noticed only then a dog sprawled before the fire, red-orange, with wild pointy ears twitching in sleep. A thick white blob of fur at the end of its tail made me start: it was in fact a fox. In the corner of my eye, two hands, graceful and white, cupped round the wheel, until it stopped still. They belonged to a woman sitting astride it, who was gazing at a ball of thread spun at her feet. The folds of her dress, aquamarine and shimmering like water, were silvered from the darkness framed in the window beside her.

"What are you doing?" I may have asked or thought. She looked over at me, her jade-green eyes shining in welcome; a mass of auburn locks spilling over her shoulders, with flecks of gold captured from the firelight. "Doing? Spinning thread for the loom that weaves all stories in the Library of Time – of which I am guardian," was her answer, delivered in a mellifluous voice, neither high nor low. It carried an authority that made me want to listen.

"And me – what am I doing here, with you?" I wondered aloud, a little stunned by her matter-of-fact declaration that was far from ordinary.

"You are here dreaming me into being."

"I am?"

"Indeed you are! I am here, as your creation."

"You don't exist in your own right?"

"Nothing exists in its own right. I am weaving your life into being as you dream me."

"My life? You can't do that – it's mine. I decide how it unfolds. I don't want your interference, thank you."

"Oh really?" she asked playfully, leaning forwards, apparently excited at the challenge and petulance in my voice. "You might change your mind when you see how well we've been doing. This way – come, follow me," she beckoned breezily, ushering me out of the room into a maze of whitewashed corridors and doorways. "I measure time's passing in bundles of colour; eons of it," she explained, guiding me through what I had assumed was a tiny cottage – yet, in a rustle of fabric, she must have swept through a mansion of rooms, my trailing behind her, so long did it take to open and shut doors; every room the same, filled with rolls of all sizes, murals and friezes, until at last we reached the one housing the story of my life.

Inside, the walls were lined with records just like all the others. The woman explained they chronicled everything that had ever happened to me, including events still to happen; the story of my birth, the different incidents of note, everyone I had ever met, friends, strangers, teachers and relatives, deaths, struggles, rewards and opportunities.

Beholding the Library of Time, I felt a giddying sense of possibilities and variables. The woman's words flowed into a seamless discourse on her vocation as 'the Weaver', as she called herself. "Everything, past and future, has been told and recorded by me. You have lived every tale of heartbreak and triumph, and every shade in between; even outcomes and eventualities you don't realise have already been created. 'Once upon a time' is really 'once there was and once there was not and will never be because it hasn't yet happened as something remembered.' You with me? Everything, all of it, is a story – with all the juice and barrenness for it to be experienced in unending variety: the play of you and me, you within your world, with him or her, doing this and trying that – your every thought, move, whim and choice are nothing more than the true and not true."

It was disconcerting beholding the static records of my entire life history and future – as inevitabilities or probabilities frozen in time. What the Weaver had said was preposterous but somehow felt true. Even the room was not what it seemed, apparently expanding, reams of rolled-up histories and futures appearing wherever my eyes roamed or settled.

"You are in the influence of the eclipse. No ordinary moment in time. It is in fact a window of chance – an opening through which, if you dare to choose, unforeseen possibilities can be claimed. You can create your destiny: a very special story with nothing predictable about it because it has never existed before – it's uniquely yours, waiting outside the known dimension of time and place."

I nodded at the scrolls. "You mean, one of those starts to play out – as some sort of new script for my life story?"

"No," she answered, holding my gaze in excitement. "I mean the opposite. A new identity that I have not yet told or foreseen – emerging in this only opportunity – a gap in time's flow. The eclipse is that passing chance, as the moon stands directly between the sun and the Earth, blocking out all reflected light in a time of pregnant darkness. Call it a threshold into the unknown! It happens rarely – it is your chance."

"My chance for what?"

"To become the dream! To live out a story that could never be imagined – to create an original masterpiece, drawing from the nectar of the most divine kingdom ever to be remembered for never having been lived or told."

"So I no longer need you! This is my chance to create this unlived story – for myself?"

"It is true I have run out of inspiration. It is yours to discover. But we need each other, you see. I need a heroine: one who blazes with fierce courage to experience territories never before imagined. And I then inscribe them, immortalising the story throughout time!"

"And what happens if I don't go through the window?"

"Then you destroy your deepest wish to drink from the chalice and know blissful fulfilment."

A log fell, showering sparks up the chimney as new embers glowed gold. A shadow fell over her. The Weaver sighed theatrically, and turned her attention to the rows of rolled-up life stories, her eyes scanning them. "This one here best illustrates the creative stalemate we have reached. In it lies another tale: your heart prompting you into the unknown," she whispered. Her long prehensile fingers gripped the edge of a scroll, allowing it to unfurl to the floor, ablaze with colour. There was a menagerie of tiny birds framed in branches, their wings delicate folds – vulnerable and courageous fledglings, facing their first flight. "This story charts the impulse inside you – to sing a song, your own song of your deepest desires to be expressed: joy, play, and beauty, plain and simple. The birdsong captured here had made you stop still and listen one springtime walk. The little songbirds were out in force, chirruping their hearts out as if their gift was to be heard for the last time. And in a sense it was – because had you not been there to listen, they wouldn't have been heard. They came alive through you, and awoke a hidden life inside you. The melodies they had sung were about life and its creations being equal. The birds are arboreal minstrels, to wake up the world to the magic of song. Your heart yearns to set free the songbird within it. Opening the window into the unknown promises trials in return for the gift – the only gift that can eclipse all torment to its attainment."

"And that gift is only received in the unknown – " I asked, "a place inspiring the little birds?"

"Venturing through the gap in time's flow can lead to that very gift – the gift of song to be brought back to the world of time, fresh and bold, uniquely your own, arousing all the other little birds to sing back in chorus."

Recalling those birds that had inspired me, I could feel that same fresh vitality springing up in me – light and bright. I wondered what would happen if I ignored my impulse to discover the unknown. The Weaver's demeanour then changed; she was suddenly pale and sad, her dress dulled of its watery sheen. "If you fail to claim your destiny, you will wander forever in the most barren desert, a hell starved of heartfelt dreams and all their colour, " she warned. "Such a fate is best explained by the cracked mirror story." The Weaver held my gaze as she resumed; other times she seemed to peer through me, to some faraway world, her voice slow and emphatic.

"There was once a girl who forgot but was always remembered. She had been raised as a baby in nature, after her mother abandoned her as a newborn in the densest forest, ashamed to beget her out of marriage. Until she could toddle around on her dimpled legs to explore the world about her, she was fed and kept safe by beings of nature, the animals, birds and spirits. Even when her life changed, being adopted by a farmer and his wife who found her, the love the wild guardians felt for the child followed her. They never forgot her – only, as she grew up, she did not remember them.

Over the years, nature was always calling out to be noticed, to remind the girl of her unique nurturing during the early years of her life. One day, as she was cleaning indoors, a branch started to rap-rap-rappety-rap against the window. She rose from her seat to look out. Opening the window, a fresh draught brushed her cheek like a kiss. And then the breeze changed into a furious wind, howling, until the house shook, as if its foundations were uprooting. The cinders she'd been sweeping lifted up from their neat piles and began to dance about the room. As they swirled, so did the maiden, chasing them about with her broom. They might stop, and then so would she, lifting the broom to sweep them up. They would begin all over again, a chaos of movement, lunging and jiving, tumbling and soaring. The maiden felt flushed with the joy of disrupted routine – giggling at the unruly piles that refused to be swept away. This went on, and how quickly time passed in play, the girl unable to get her work done.

When her parents returned from the fields, the cinders were strewn around the parlour. They told her off for being lazy. When she explained how they had scattered and dodged her brushstrokes, a will of their own, they got angry. She had been carried away by a flight of fancy. Cinders didn't dance – anyone knew that!

From that day on, the maiden chose to carry about her tasks with the door and windows shut. She would block her ears if ever a branch rapped against one. Time passed, and she began to lose the skip in her step, the rose in her cheek, the song in her voice, so immersed was she in the drudge of her indoor chores. One day she saw her reflection in a hand mirror as she cleaned around it. She hadn't seen herself in a long time and paid attention to her features so often described as bonny by those who knew her. As she looked on, not unpleased, she dropped the mirror on the floor. It cracked, one clean fracture through the middle. Picking it up to see the damage, the maiden could only feel horror at what stared back at her."

The Weaver stopped abruptly. She placed her hand against her throat, looking as surprised as the heroine she described. "The reflection, as you would expect, was split in two by the crack. Only that is where all reason stops. One half of the mirror reveals a young girl's anguished face, tears streaming down her cheek. She is lost and very alone. The other is that of a haggard crone, her eyes grim and bitter with disillusionment, and face ravaged with the regret of broken dreams and hopes unrealised. The maiden sees this vision as clear as day. It then vanishes, leaving her in a most gloomy and dispirited mood." That last sentence was delivered by the Weaver in a tone of finality. I stared on, expecting her to continue but she didn't.

"And then? What does she do after that," I urged, uncomfortable with the silence filling the room.

"Nothing. That's what she sees and that's where the story ends."

"What – ends there? What kind of story is that? Surely, she has to find out what the mirror was showing her."

"She saw what the mirror showed her."

"Yes, and then what? Who was the crying girl, the worn old woman? Why did they appear before the Maiden? Mirrors don't just crack!"

"Oh really?" The Weaver looked at me with all the patience of a sympathetic parent. "It can be so. There does not have to be an ending that is logical or in any way satisfactory."

"But I want the Maiden to wake up – to find out about the mystery behind the mirror. It's clearly a call to leave her boring home, wander around, discover... like all heroes in the myths must do."

"That may be your idea of a story," the Weaver said, her glittering eyes holding mine with unnerving clarity. "But for this young lady, and others like her, there is no such impulse. Countless heroes and heroines, such as yourself, have tasted adventure, exploring the surface of the Earth in all its directions. But as the Weaver, the record keeper of every story lived and to be lived, I can assure you there is only one direction the story should take if it doesn't end at disappointment."

"Where?"

"A true heroine must choose a different journey: the verticality of descent."

"Down? I know about down! Where could that lead this time?"

"Into the despair of your deepest disappointment – through the crushing terror of never having lived your fullest, fiercest, bravest and most passionate life – with all the rage and tears, sweetness and laughter of heartbreak. You will be crushed, sacrificed, die again and again at the altar of your own making."

"And how do I get down there? And what then – how does it end?"

"The eclipse will help you find out. It is the gateway – to empower your descent."

"And then?"

Only there was no then to be revealed. I somehow woke up, my mouth dry and thirsty. I got up, turned off the heating and headed to the kitchen for some water. Settling back to bed, no matter how vividly I recalled the Weaver's last words, I couldn't dive back in to the dream, to find out what happened next. I felt strangely awake, despite feeling worn out as though I'd actually lived every detail of our intensely lucid encounter. There was no reasonable way to figure out the next steps – when 'descent' ended and how long it had to be endured. I felt a flash of fear imagining the darkness, lost and alone, swallowed up in something I couldn't handle. Grandmother had said I had to feel my way into the hell of pain, the fear and sadness, the depths of the unknown housed at Mount Bugarach. And the Weaver spoke of a window of chance supporting my journey – the eclipse. That was today. I remembered its synchronicity with the fertility rite in Egypt, thousands of years before – this very eclipse regarded as an auspicious time to sow seeds and create anew. The heavenly alignment could also inspire me – helping to charge my own intention for a fresh start.

I yawned. It was comforting being snug in the narrow single bed, breathing in the cool night air, the window open ajar. As my mind slowed, my body felt heavier, sinking into the mattress with each deepening breath. On the sweet cusp of slumber, the last thing I remember was the rap-rap-rappety-rap of a branch against my bedroom window.

Chapter 5

Into the Spiral

At the edge of the river, using a stick to balance my weight, I leapt across the shallowest dam of stones to the other side. Straggly branches and wild bramble pricked me, as I cleared a way on to another trail running parallel to the mountain's base. The verge steepened into a ravine, the river coursing along it. The other side, Mount Bugarach looked alive with movement – twisting, swirling patterns a measure of its evolution. Faces within the rock took form, peering out through the gulf separating us as natural sculptures ravaged by time and climate. Everywhere was a harmony of rock and water, a vitality of green springing from stone.

As I got closer, the distinctive splice that had so inspired my route for the day looked a perfect backdrop for mythical drama, as if it might yield a passage into the womb of the mountain. Intentions on a new moon had the power of nature behind them. And there I was, remembering my own, the reason for being out in the gloom, while beholding something that resembled a chalice, or the life-giving apparatus of a mothering force. I wanted to transform whatever stopped me from feeling at peace in my own skin.

Without venturing further, it was impossible to know if there was a cave or opening within the gash. The mountain was bound to harbour surprises for anyone persistent enough to explore its every suggestion of access. It was tempting to find out for myself – but being on Bugarach's wilder side and with the prospect of rain, I felt more cautious. Time could disappear quickly, so it was best to press on. Unlike the well-worn path and softer gradient the other side, the way I was going, with its cliffs and greater exposure, could become quickly treacherous in poor visibility.

The cloud thinned for a moment. The lower mountain lit up and creased with shadow. Farmhouses dotted along the valley would be exposed to the same eerily spectacular views. I dropped through the trees to scout out a route across the swollen river. It had flooded up to a gate leading to woods and lower pastures. I threw a boulder to help break my leap across. One foot missed, landing firmly in the cold water, which made swift work of my waterproofed boot.

Beyond the gate, the atmosphere changed again. Weaving my way through silvery saplings, I felt energised with adventure. Soggy and content, I trudged towards fields of grazing sheep and goat. Rocks and boulders scattered over the lower pastures looked propped against each other too seamlessly to have happened accidentally. Perhaps they had been dislodged by a tremor or outflow during the volcano's primordial past – but closer up, they could have been the remains of ancient dwellings or summer shelters of shepherds. I sensed the imprints of human tread, a resonance of old pathways – the first herders and settlers would have had countless ways up the mountain. There were piles of rocks and stones dotting a route to the summit, but I was feeling drawn along faint goat trails traversing the slope.

The energy grew noticeably stronger. My stomach responded – and a surge of adrenaline made me aware of my racing heartbeat. My senses were sharper – the river's force still audible, far below my pounding steps, the greens more vivid, every rock strikingly unique, a bird's call responding to another. This was how a pioneer must feel – as alive as I felt right then – making new tracks, preferring the path less trodden. A real fresh start, rather than a half-hearted one, was what I craved for my own life. My resolve had to be bolder than the compelling instinct to live by what I'd known. I could no longer ignore the pattern of enthusiasm followed by despondency that would erupt, no matter how good my life looked. Nothing terrible had ever happened to explain a lurking anxiety that I wasn't living my best life. I had to know what that best life could be – if it was possible to be truly fulfilled.

Over my shoulder the main route up looked a lot more direct than the softer incline I followed. Just a short distance apart, and it was like crossing another threshold among Bugarach's many faces. A protruding spine of rock like a scaly dragon's tail carved up the slope in front. The fall from it to the valley floor was impressive. The geology this side of the mountain was more extreme, evoking the Earth as primal matter, bubbling and cooling, thrusting and collapsing in the extremes of cool and heat. Considering such evolution inspired a sense of scale that pulped the absurdity of my self-importance. The rock vividly testified life's endless expansion – reducing me to being nothing more than a particle of organic transience beside the mountain's forbearance, weathered over millions of years. I felt awed imagining it as a volcano, a volatile force of fire – a mere eye-blink ago in creation's measureless scale. The story of time was held within its strata. Through ancient eyes, all matter began its journey of transformation through fire. A place fertile with stories – such as an 'Upside Down Mountain' – was bound to have a mythical geology, a landscape guarded by a fire-breathing dragon, such as the one I beheld!

The bouldered spine towered over me, spectacular and indifferent, compelling me to explore it. I could balance on some rocks, skipping between them, and scrambled along others. Its jagged edges resembled gothic archways and steeples. Such perfect proportions within all nature were replicated from the cell to the sunflower, within rocks and skeletons, petals and wings. Such building blocks were universal – evident in the microscopic particle and vaster cosmos, following geometrical archetypes that also inspired sacred architecture and structures. Wherever I looked were perfect ovals, circles, squares and rectangles, the same core shapes used in human design – to inspire devotion and worship. In the roofless temple of

Bugarach, there could be no refuge from a dangerous world, with all its unforgiving exposure. The damp fog and breeze were prodding me awake – as if to disarm the layers of conditioning and comfort buffeting my own elemental nature.

I was beginning to feel overwhelmed by all the space. Balance, poise and nerve were essential ingredients for climbing. Right then, nearing an edge of the dragon's tail and the drop beyond it, I was physically free and unhindered. A flat grassy patch was just big enough to lie on my front with my head craning over the drop, level with the choughs gliding far above the shrub. Up there, I too could have been airborne. A hawk's vision could eye the edible detail, a mouse, rabbit, among that beautiful blur of browns, greys and greens hundreds of feet below. This must be what it was to really fly, relishing perspective; attending only to what mattered and soar over anything that didn't!

That was my last thought before everything changed. A crow hollered throatily. I looked up as it circled, its velveteen blue-black wings large enough to be mistaken for a hawk. It dived into the valley, just as a force began welling around me. At first, it felt like a tug, then nothing, followed by another, before gripping me in a magnetic suction. My body was immobile, lying supported by millions of tonnes of rock, and yet my experience told me something else entirely. A chasm was surely opening up beneath me: I felt weightless, somehow held by the gravity of the mountain's mass. It wasn't just its density I could sense, but a force of unfathomable power that could mince me within its grinding weight.

Images and thoughts streamed within my mind. A spiral like a corkscrew wound from the depths into the endless above. It was luminous, piercing through the rock's solidity, and on upwards into the engulfing gloom. At each twist a threshold glimmered, etheric and unstable. Wherever I placed my attention, a door would open, to reveal spectacular panoramas the other side – desert, sea, cloudscape, mountain range or jungle. This was crazy – how could this be happening given the solid ground beneath me? Any such doubt only accelerated the giddying movement, calling me to witness. My body was being pulled to merge with the spiral's centrifugal force, a helter-skelter of garish neon swirling in both directions.

Round I went, nauseous with the motion, faster and faster until I hovered above a gaping shaft, inviting me to let go, to plunge for the ride to somewhere unknown and unseen. I wasn't ready, and focused instead on the doors within the spiral that opened up to people, faces, ages, times, scenes and places. They were all related to me in some way, as familiar as allies, even those I couldn't recognise. Circling downwards, I was unable to break free of the suction pulling out my every thought, churning around a confusion of theories, questions and doubts in giddying force. There was nothing recognisable to focus upon. I was being severed from everything and everyone I had ever known – nothing more than a husk, alone and loveless, haunted in exile.

Overwhelmed, I started to burrow for a way out of my misery. This was how a rat would feel, wired to survive. I sensed a faint tremor in the rocks, a pulse like a slowed heartbeat – deep and primal. It made me imagine an inseparable maternal force ushering in all life, causing everything within its field to cry out for its first breath, reaching out for touch, for contact in the stark alien glare and crush of time and place – the physical dimension where sensuous wonder or hell will determine the ride. Or was that very pulse, so ancient and familiar, the rain – pitter-pattering on the mineral solidity of the overhang where I lay sprawled? As each drop splattered, I was pushed deeper into black space.

Drop, drop, drop, did not feel liquid-wet – more the hard coldness of metal; drop-drop-drop could have been the snip-snip, snippety-snip of scissors, cutting and shredding in functional persistence. The rhythm was becoming more urgent, a ripping and slashing through heaps of rags by large blades in heartless ceremony. They were once my outfits, the many costumes worn for a variety of roles. As they fell, I was freed of them, stark and exposed. As quickly as they went, more appeared – a burlesque of frill and colour, a blur of shapes and sizes accentuating the curves and contours of my womanhood. I stared on: at the discarded fragments of my life – who was clutching the shears, behind the every rip, slice and shred?

A black blob shimmered among the bundle – it had spindly desiccated legs, eight of them. It was a spider's carapace! Spiders terrified me, for their sudden, unpredictable scuttle. As long as they didn't move, I could see, with some imagination, how they might be beautiful. Beholding this one didn't make me scream: it was inseparable from the clothes and outfits that were once me. The primal pulse became louder, wearyingly persistent. The carapace was like an iridescent silk of blue-green, shot with crimson. It was the emerging form of a familiar woman, ageless and beautiful, and as I wondered who she might be, her face disappeared – leaving me with a hint of something indefinable, a frustrating slip away from being memorable. I waited, knowing she'd come back, as the spiral twisted on. At last she returned and took shape, her hands and arms an entrancing blur as she breathed the spiral into life. A mysterious force was taking life through her hands; colourful threads transferring from each of her dancing limbs, animating in the spiral between us as the content of my life story, a journey through vast distances.

"Are we creating this together?" I wondered – recognising the spiral as a fantastical flavour of my life, not all rooted in direct experience; an infinite band of colour and romp through the physical dimension of time and space – a circus troupe of exotic ephemera, sequinned elephants and flying carpets, giant dragonflies and Persian cats, whirling dervishes, murky tarns in heathery Highland slopes, herbs and potions with the promise of magic, spices and fragrances, the blind beggar who I had spotted in markets and city squares all over the world, West and East, who saw into the future, the Gypsy busker, and Tibetan monk whose corrugated iron home sheltered me from deluge one monsoon.

A stream of scenes shifted and flickered into life, until one grew out from the others the more I focused on it – a garden springing as a surprise from behind thick oaks and holly bush. There was an irresistible magic to its rose-beds, box hedges and blooming borders, and also the unusual house beyond it – with old russet bricks, leaded windows framed in timber, a disused pump in a corner, and tower at one end, a feature as familiar as myself. It would have overlooked the coastal farmland where the sea once lapped. It was St Margaret's Priory. I was born there. I was named after it too. Margaret.

I must have made that same approach to the house from the woods hundreds or thousands of times. I sighed at its welcome, a sanctuary harbouring the ghosts of my own history and those from its passage through the centuries. I noted the windows of the room where I was delivered safely into the world, named after the sun – the solar. It took up most of the first floor behind two chimney breasts, each with three tall stacks. The space between them resembled glowing sceptres against a sunlit sky. Its majesty, I could see, wasn't about grandeur or elegant proportions – the charm too ramshackle and eccentric for that; inside were secret passages and bedrooms as corridors, wood-panelled rooms and hidden recesses. It was never a priory; one owner bolted on the monastic flourish. It didn't need such extras: I could feel the building as radiantly powerful as a living being – bricks, wood and stone with spirit.

The 'Priory' was an unlikely hideaway between two encroaching cities, a place of imagination and rampage for four girls growing up. Even in adulthood it remained my one true 'home', my parents living on there. There was something else to be seen, hidden in the heartfelt sentiment; a sinister edge to my attachment that I hadn't before faced. My presence at the house was not only inevitable. There was a force field binding me within its very fabric; my future arrested in the building's history. I was captured as an eternal child, with its 'little sister' identity forged there. From childhood to the present day, a whirl of my fast-paced life emanated out into the world from within its walls – the growing up and travel, different addresses and pursuits, boyfriends, studies, jobs. Throughout testing times 'the Priory' had been a beacon, as well as its trusted guardians, my parents and unwavering allies; so many triumphs shared under that roof too, many celebrations and gatherings of friends. The spiral was confronting me with something more: as much as I was sheltered and loved there, escape was part of its tower-top refuge, an exile of my own-making. When the grit of life wore me down, I could withdraw and forget, give up for a while until I was ready to re-enter the race. What a gift – and one with a cost. 'The Priory', for all its nostalgia, inspired me to dream, safe and held – but I could never quite break free from its magnetism that made it so much more than a draughty old building, a house of touching memories, that had inspired my name.

Margaret no-middle-name MacKean, the bank of names exhausted on three other girls already. And there was an honour enjoyed being born in the home my parents so loved and named me after. I had an unrivalled connection to the place among my siblings. Three decades on, the spiral showed me tucked away in the tower writing – disciplined days and long months of solitary labour, always between projects and destinations, returning to record such ventures in its arboreal silence. Story after story, always one unifying theme: Margaret dreaming of the comforting finishing line when everything neatly tied up, and life beyond St Margaret's Priory was finally as it should be, a liberated Rapunzel with the fortune of everything 'worked out'. The longing for the all-accepting, ever-exciting Mr Right and rejection of Mr Wrong in all his guises was part of that dream, an impetus for a rescue that would one day free me from my lonely search, and all its disappointment – the looking out among the nesting birds from the windows of my study, wondering when the arrival of my perfect future and adoring chaperone through it would finally show up. Until that day, my life was driven by meaningful endeavour, with lofty heights to scale, and rewards for their attainment. Only even that lifeline slipped away – no longer tethering me to hope in a faraway moment of landing somewhere right and solid.

Tap, tap, tap – the pitter-patter of rain – as gentle and persistent as the fluttering wing-beat of a bird taking off, gaining speed. The Priory faded as it seemed to fall away – perhaps it was the sound of my own wings beating, rising me up to somewhere else. Where next within the spiral? It glimmered in my vision as the vista shrank, swallowed in thick grey. Even the river along the mountain's base I couldn't see. Its flow seemed louder than before, funnelled upwards by a gust sweeping through the valley like a wave. Lone raindrops fell, each one splattering audibly with a 'plop' – reminding me of the perfect pitch metal makes swung into hard blue ice. Before me ice crystals glistened, reflecting a rainbow of light within a square of white. I could feel the intensity of my focus, my life depending on that unwavering concentration and commitment of my every muscle – limbs shaking with the effort of exertion. One swing – 'plop', then another – 'plop'.

I was back in a moment in which the serrated edges of axe and crampon were the only connection to dubious solidity. Ice climbing was a knife-edge flirt with danger. It woke me up, like nothing before or since – not sheer walls of rock with their nicks and grooves, faint handholds for a route upwards. Rope attached to real earth had kept me safe – always a lifeline if the gravity got too much, and fingers started to slide, knuckles whitening, my whole body trembling and sweaty from the grip, weight and fear; then a fall, rock rising, a plunging stomach, but never full abandon to chance, for at some point the drop would be slowed by the elasticity of rope; nothing too jolting, perhaps a juddery bounce, only a play of consequences rarely life-threatening. The icy realms were quite different. They demanded more surrender. The greater the risk, the more skill and resolve required. There was less give or take at altitude, less negotiation with danger. It brought me into the freedom of each and every moment – placing an unreasonable faith in the inherently unstable world of frozen water. Until even that faith, that passionate faith, couldn't hold me any longer – crashing once and for all in New Zealand.

High and alone on an ice-wall there, my legs were shaking violently. My hands were gripping the ice axes so tightly my arms ached, lower back tightening against the unyielding drag of gravity. Hundreds of feet below, my friend was waiting. He looked so small in the icy vastness – but I had to forget that, my attention only on my next move to get ready to follow him. I could feel his impatience, radiating upwards in the eerie still silence, the sun beating down from cloudless skies in a hell of glaring cold. The panorama, hundreds of glaciated peaks encircling us in the legendary Mount Cook National Park, would have been heavenly if I hadn't been blinded by fear. Instead, the dazzling beauty, and its pristine crystal clarity, cold and mocking, charged that fear – so out of place in a realm where Gods would live.

Everything still. Unbearably still. Such weight in the silence. My next move not forthcoming, only a screaming tension at life hovering, waiting for me to move, everything suspended until the next muscular twitch that would hint there was will in me yet. My neck felt rigid, my helmeted head the heaviest burden. The pop and crackle of ice crystals softening in the sun was getting louder now I listened. I risked glancing over my shoulder: everywhere light captured within glistening seracs, walls of rainbow-filled diamonds. My breath was held. I freed it – deliberately taking in slow deep breaths, the air so dry my throat was sore with searing thirst. We'd been going for hours – risking the arduous walk – out in the eighteen hours of daylight available. There was no Plan B. This was the last basin to descend, the last technical challenge.

Gavin had done it – smooth and effortless. Seamless movements, hypnotic rhythm of blade on snow – steady and persistent – plop, plop of each blade, crunch, crunch of the kicking crampons. One axe in, the other out, one crampon freed, lowered, and then the next. Watching him, I knew I could do it – that I had to do it. Rope wasn't an option for that height anyway. There would only have been enough to belay me half the wall at most. Safety in such isolation had to be measured against narrow weather windows, situated within a lick of the southern ocean, the stormiest region on Earth. Once he reached flat solid ice, I had to follow – what other choice was there? His red jacket was like a drop of blood in all the white.

The swing and rhythm was usually enjoyable, its momentum quickly lulling me into unquestioned commitment with the only task in hand: each single moment, frame by frame, my vision locked on the white square in front. But something felt different, almost at once. I wasn't losing myself to a sense of flow or instinct. I had placed myself in an alien situation, painfully aware of every rising thought and doubt, never forgetting the unnatural exposure, the two hundred foot fall should my grip give, or ice break. The pack could flip me over like a turtle – all thirty kilos of it. Curse the snowshoes! We hadn't used them once. Eight kilos, ten? And we were a helicopter ride from the nearest human or prospect of rescue.

There, stranded, no longer focused or present, the full unforgiving price of my hubris paralysed me. The facts: I was scared of heights and as restless as I'd ever been. What was more, the truth had been nagging at me for long stressful months, which I had hidden from my peers, and barely acknowledged myself. To admit such weakness would allow the genie to escape. What then? Where would that open door lead? My whole life constructed around endeavour, the quest for achievement, was as miserable and empty as it ever was. I'd forsaken the career ladder for one at altitude – and nothing had really changed. Only this time, in this graphic moment being relived, months of doubt and uncertainty were overwhelming me without mercy. Fear rose unchecked. I was cramped in the torment of pause, rigid and stunned. Something had to move. It was too late for regrets. I couldn't be rescued.

– "How you doing up there, Mags?"

Gavin's voice sounded feeble, pathetic in the dry crisp air, brittle in the vast space separating us from normal life, from cars and people. A strand of iced hair was bothering me – straying into my mouth, but to flick it away would mean a greater level of trust in the blades holding my weight. "Mags?" he persisted.

God I wanted to scream at him – rage at the pent-up loathing and fear being so alone, my friend having underestimated my experience, leading me on an 'adventure of a lifetime', his long-held dream, allowing his own ambition to override the pretence of mine. I could feel his regret, his anxiety in the countdown to nightfall, of our limited water, and rising thirst – no running water at these heights – his keen awareness of my slowing down, my fatigue – my inability to do anything at all. I was frozen still! And my legs wouldn't respond, my body locked. Nothing could move. "Breathe," I sighed aloud. That was the only thing I could do – choose to breathe. One more time – again, breathe! Focus on the white in front of my nose, I willed. Don't look down. Don't answer. None needed. Legs still quivering, arms aching. Slowing down was lethal, and to stop? Momentum, I told myself, meant one move swiftly followed by another. It was the only way to dance down ice. Staccato-like efforts were a force of resolve, exhausting to maintain.

One blade out – heavy in the air. No time to think where best to place it. Plop! In it went, the angle awkward, forcing me to twist and push out my arse. It was the last thing I wanted – desperate to lean flat against the ice, clinging on, limiting my exposure to the icy air.

Scrunched over the lower blade, I counted to ten, knowing the higher axe had to come out.

Time slows in the hell of fear. Who knows how long Gavin had waited for me to make my way down? His frustration, barely disguised, cajoled me again and again. "Keep going," he wailed – not the kind of mantra to still my mind. Frustration was in his voice, in my grunted responses, in each weary determined move. One more swing, one more kick. And another.

It's hard to know how, but I had reached the bottom in the next scene to be witnessed. Unmoved by the begrudging "Well done", I allowed my legs their right to collapse. Just a litre left of water, between us. "Go steady," Gavin urged, handing me the bottle. We really had to get moving, he reminded. There was another ten hours of descent, he calculated, before the moraine and then roadside march to Fox, where he lived. He would have done it in six – but eight was his best guess for the two of us.

That was to prove somewhat optimistic. Fourteen hours it took for me to slump against the door, a bed the other side. But we couldn't have known that then – and such was the way of adventure. That battle down the ice, it was to turn out, was not only my last-ever ice climb, but the beginning of the longest fight I had ever faced to keep going. The prospect of rest and food was a cruel phantom, haunting our struggle through an alien world of creaking ice blocks, luminous giants in the dark. The elusive arrival prolonged the torment, each bone-aching step, every blister and yawn – all of it.

Mountaineering had been my dream. It was my ticket to a rewarding life. That last climb had emptied a reservoir of drive. I saw images of myself adrift, for long months following, as lost as I ever once was. But that was a whole other story – and my hands were getting cold. In fact all of me felt cold. The rain was thickening, slushy cold – but I hadn't finished on the dragon's edge. I spotted a patch of river reappearing as the cloud bank drifted on. Yes, it had been a tightrope since giving up climbing: playing safe had stemmed the same untameable instinct within me that was so much part of the spirit of Bugarach. Facing my fear was equally joyless – and avoiding it made me feel like an overloaded engine straining between gears. Where was the balance?

A long moment of stillness followed, as if the wind was biding its time – then a steady breeze began stirring and whipping up another labyrinth of memory. A new doorway opened up: this one a threshold to the Himalayas, encompassing vibrant turning points of my life. Many visits tied together as a karmic bundle – flashes of drama, frozen as snapshots; two austere meditation retreats, twelve days of silence to observe my breath and lurching mind; the ascent of a hostile mass of ice and rock one Nepali monsoon two weeks after the royal massacre, and a moody romance with a cousin of the doomed family, a movie star with all the strut and glamour of caricature; wilderness expeditions among the world's highest passes and summits; an immersion at an ashram to research and write among the rich mix of Hindu, Buddhists and Tibetans in exile; and the meeting of a Frenchman in a bewitchingly beautiful mountaintop setting, who looked a credible life partner until he crashed off that pedestal with violent finality.

Cartoonish clouds puffed across the Himalayan skies, the wind nostalgic and unsettling. I was feeling nauseous and feverish, stomach cramping and throat dry – my sleeping bag damp in the fuggy confinement of a tent. My brow was being mopped by him, *l'homme beau*. He was strikingly handsome. That time in the tent, I was helpless and grateful. Over several days, he had nursed me tenderly and tirelessly back to strength, finding two stray puppies to cheer me up that we fed and petted, until we could resume our long hike through remote villages and valleys of Himachal Pradesh. Our chance meeting felt so loaded with 'meant to be' – after he spotted me in a café thronged with other travellers, and admired the altimeter bulging from my wrist. His English had made no sense, and switching to French allowed me to fill in the gaps of translation with some generous embellishments. He was refreshingly irreverent and confident, eighteen years my senior – with an authority of experience and knowledge easy to admire. We had plenty in common it turned out as travelling partners – a love of the outdoors, simple Buddhist practices and the feel-good rhythm of long-distance walking.

The wind then brought me to Provence, to a solitary stone farmhouse, looking out over mountains shaped like sleeping giants. Nose and chin, eyelid and earlobe, the contours I traced became the imaginary guardians of my heart's secrets – dreaming of a wholesome, satin-and-lace marriage ahead. My French lover had proved himself an irresistible mix: both urbane and rooted in the ideals of his rustic childhood. Our relationship was as mercurial as the stifling heat and storm of those late summer weeks – vibrant times of cooking and feasting, exploring canyons, bathing in rivers, and long loving spells in the antique chestnut bed we'd moved outside, awaking each morning to the tinkling bells of goatherds migrating up the mountain. One night, cooler inside than out, we sat by a fire. His face was pinched and angry in the dimming light. I had annoyed him again, causing him to observe my nature needed maturing. It was still a little fiery and restless. I was lovely but would ripen with the help of Buddhist techniques that he had mastered. My behaviour – the questions and challenges, tensions and energy that quickly tired of passivity – excited his agitation that three decades of meditation and yoga had mostly calmed. In a few years, he could see, when my spirit was quieter, I would flower into the ideal woman I was seeded to become. In the meantime, he would support my meditation attempts and growth, and recite the dogma of Saints and Yogis who had inspired him.

Looking back, who was 'she' that I then was? What happened to the heat simmering deep inside the woman I could recognise as me, listless by the fire? Branches from a walnut tree scraped against a window, loudly enough for me to notice now. Their urgency, so obvious looking back, was to wake me up to the dangers I wasn't then ready to accept, determined to believe in the love story playing out. After all, didn't he have a point? My force of spirit and will worried me too – I was, after all, the common factor in all my failed relationships. How could I trust myself given the blind spots that others could see so clearly that slipped through my awareness, terrifying me for escaping unnoticed? He was right: I needed the guidance, the taming.

The spiral shifted to our road trip through a charm of Moroccan cities, seaside idylls and desert mountains. It was easy to track my frustration simmering over long slow mornings devoted to meditation, my body twitching with eagerness to move and explore. How haunting the wail of the call to prayer each dawn, reminding me of the torturous hours ahead before we would emerge outside and feel the new day. In one snapshot, meditating together, I saw myself opening an eye, to check if he was still there, so silent and empty the bedroom space had become. His face was reposed and inscrutable, as it had been when I last peeked; posture rock-still, a veritable limpet of unwavering intent. Over the three weeks, I could feel his frustration uncurling as a snake ready to strike, increasingly sensitive to my impatience and whims. Each day, his opinions were more emphatic – there was a right way of doing things, such as adapting the driver's seat for my shorter legs every time it was my turn to take over. Or was the trigger the row which flared after I drove over a stray cat that sprinted across the road? Tearful, I had tried to forget the regrettable shudder of its body squashed beneath the wheels. This was, he pointed out, something he would never have done. It was a loss of control. He spoke in all the coolness of repressed anger – later to unleash in the heat of rage. The fast-moving pace was whipping up our already volatile chemistry – the fallouts and reluctant apologies. And at last – a row over money – in which I refused to pay for the shoes he wanted as a gesture of gratitude for using his car for the trip.

Whack! – the explosive *gifles* and the sting of those two sharp slaps across my cheeks. A pause between each one – not long enough for him to register surprise and regret. How rage could shrink the face of someone uncommonly kind and trusting – his large blue eyes narrowing and darkened in grim detachment. The wind had persisted, tailing us on the long sea voyage back to Marseilles; in the spiral, I could hear myself shutting it out, struggling to keep hopeful. "I must make this work, I must!"

How many other past loves had served their role in my catastrophic breakdown with romance? Frustration, I had discovered, was an inevitable part of intimacy – a painful torment of crushed hopes and regrets. Hadn't the quest for 'the one', the magician to save me with worlds of unimaginable marvel, been the same drive to seek answers and distractions – a quest for meaning and the climb ever upwards, to the ultimate realm of one-day happiness, far above the density of disappointment?

Still I marched on, round and round the spiral's unending twists and turns. The breeze that had whipped up uncomfortable memories now blew into my face, inducing unbearable nausea. It was the persistent shake of the shaman's 'chakapa', a fan of leaves to brush away and redirect the unwanted energies seeping out of my body. An exotic cacophony of jungle sound and otherworldly medicine songs collided into an overbearing instinct to purge my guts out, to excavate the discomfort held within every cell of my being. All beginning and end had no meaning. I was shapeless, without body, just a swamp of rotting, fetid refuse that couldn't be released from any orifice going quickly enough. Each of my cells was a microcosm of infinite intelligence, a universe of possibility.

Deeper the purge took me until I merged with every shade of green in the thick lushness, to hold every plant, tree, insect, butterfly and dragonfly within an enveloping fever of vital music that I had become – the creaking trees, the buzz and hum of insects, birdsong, frog-song, the howl of predator and shrieking prey. All around me, life and death were entwined so vividly: trees falling for more light for new life, parasitic relationships of creeping vines and tendrils, lichen and fungi thriving in moist and damp, the rotting, mulching decay that devoured homes of thatched leaf, bamboo and wood within three months of standing empty. Everywhere was a frenzy of life, teeming with knowledge and medicines. And there in my field of vision was the mother plant of them all, *ayahuasca*. The Vine of the Soul. One gulp of the bitter-tasting brew could be enough to open up such realms usually accessed in death.

"Hold on for the ride," I told myself, as the images and sensations intensified, plunging me deeper into darkness. The jungle gathered me and lifted me high into the sky. It took me up and up until I reached the vaulted chamber of a heavenly nursery. I was the unending innocence of an enchanted childhood shimmering with pastel hues and the fine vibration of enveloping angel wings. The luminous ones were my guardians. Each night they would tuck me up in a four-poster bed plumped high with pillows and untie a lace shroud to seal me within a world of innocent dreams.

Only I was becoming tired of that dream, and all the peering through portals and doorways, of times past and remembered – to face the depths of being I most wanted to avoid. The effort of trying to be someone else – making myself better, wiser, smarter – was catching up. Even passion could become exhausting. Where was the exception? Hadn't I witnessed it somewhere – a shrine of heart-centred simplicity and peace?

The shelter that I had seen at the beginning of the spiral. An age ago. It took life again, emanating a quiet I could feel through the veils of time at Mount Bugarach. The monk who lived there never seemed to leave his tiny plot. As I used to stride past, up and down the pine-covered valley to interview his fellow exiled Tibetans, the hunched old man would nod at me, a wordless feature of every day during a two-month stay at McLeod Ganj. One day, his face lit up as I passed him perched on a log outside his front door. It was early afternoon when the monsoon began to pour. Ushering me inside, he pointed to a rolled-up mattress, where I took my place. There were only the necessities of one spoon, knife and fork, one bowl and plate, one pan and camping stove, a sack of rice and dried beans. The concrete floor looked recently swept. The saucepan banged as it boiled, to which he added two heaped teaspoons of tea and a splash of tinned milk. Silently we sat as the rain pounded on the roof like gravel, the birdsong drowned out as the trees took the first hit of rain. Time stretched.

For decades he'd been in this same spot, thousands of miles from Tibet. He would have been among the first wave of refugees refusing to renounce the sovereignty of their homeland to the Chinese storming Lhasa. What would desperation feel like, choosing to leave the land they cherished, to trudge along hazardous mountain passes to the alien refuge of India? Like all those exiles, he would have faced the ravaging winds and frozen wastes with a pathetic armoury of plastic shoes and yak wool jumpers, heart fierce with freedom. I tried to imagine such a choice: to endure months risking frostbite, snow blindness, exhaustion, starvation and recapture – forsaking Tibet that it could live on unblemished in memory, as the new rulers brutalised the will of loved ones left behind.

As we had sipped our tea, I noticed him clasping a tin cup, the fingers of his hand gnarled by frostbite. Every time we caught eyes, he broke into a big smile and "aahed" and "eed" – agreeing to whatever I might have been thinking. Most of the time we looked out at the rain soaking the valley in contented silence. Among the tangle of plants and trees was a splash of pink. A wild rose. The petals and their delicate overlay looked lit up in the monsoon's green fluorescence. I heard "aah" and noticed the monk smiling at my surprise. This rose was an unlikely treasure hidden in the shadows – there all along, brought to life only when it was seen. He nodded and "aahed" enthusiastically until he doubled back and laughed, as if his belly couldn't relax until every single giggle ever trapped there had expressed. I laughed with him – what else was there to do? Soon we were both howling until the tears streamed down our faces. Quite what was funny was unclear and it didn't matter. We were diving into a moment as unending as it was ordinary.

Out of the blue, the weight of memory began wrenching me down through a density of feeling. An echo ricocheted like a deafening chant: "The way up is down! Up is down!" Within the mountain, a tidal wave of anything unexpressed was waiting to be remembered. Unresolved energy was seeking form. I was whirling through a hallway of mirrors. There were thousands of reflections mirroring back every aspect of who I was. They wore every possible shade of human disposition – a spectrum from angelic to the demonic – power-crazed and enfeebled, courageous and meek, passionate and frigid, glowingly truthful and pretending, embodying sham and deceit. I was lost in a labyrinthine hallway, following the way up without exit. I knew with certainty that every face looking back at me, the every variety of being I beheld was me. Every single one, the ghoulish and beautiful, was in fact me – we were one and the same!

"Don't think," I managed to think. Confusion is in thinking. I can't think my way into my heart. Oh God I'm lost in a cat-and-mouse chase of continual seeking. Where is the way out of here? Who on earth am I? My vision – everything I perceived – was nothing more than an arrow, firing outwards, into the world outside of me. At some point in its trajectory, the arrow would recoil back to the only place it could ever stop, to the source of its journey: myself. Everywhere I looked and turned was nothing more than a shimmering mirror reflecting the expanded, whole self. All resistance, doubt and judgment had to be projected on to this cast of thousands, dissolving as soon as every wretched, lonely face, the brightest and darkest, was fully welcomed back to the one home where they all belonged – me! Like hungry ghosts, they were waiting to be reclaimed, accepted for what they were, within an infinite Hallway of Mirrors, like a library of selves. They had to return to the one place holding the only truth of who I am, that is within me, and nowhere to be found outside of me.

No sooner than I had that epiphany, a row of doorways lined up in the spiral. I knew them to be thresholds to my former escape. Each one had a sign emblazoned across it: "Priory." "Climbing." "Romance." "Amazon." "Tibet."

"Are you recognising the theme of your story?" a voice pealed out.

"Is that you, Grandmother?" I answered.

"You are facing the exile of your own making – but there is further to journey. You have to feel your way through every disappointment living on in those other times and places – until you reach the other side."

"What do I have to do differently this time?"

"Awareness is the first step. Acceptance the next. Only when you embrace each feeling can the key turn at every doorway to the beyond. You have yet to cross over to the other side."

Silence. The spiral had gone. There was nothing there.

A low roar of distant thunder had brought me back – back to the rocky slope on Bugarach where I had been lying down. Some way away, a storm belt was blackening everything in its wake. Everything about me looked just as it did, the gloom still obscuring the upper mountain. It was too soon to make any

Chapter 6

Mother Shell, Daughter Shell

I slowly rose to my feet, without glancing over the edge close to where my head had been. Stepping back, I jumped up and down and stamped my feet to feel grounded. I had to scramble back along the dragon's tail before traversing the slope to descend along the trail to the village. Striding forwards, I felt energised and lucid despite the fullness of the last half hour that had opened up vast terrains within me. There was a nagging urge to get a bit higher before heading back – to get a sense of the route to the summit for another day, and see what lay beyond every hump encountered. Higher up, the clouds were still too low to get a view. I turned around to look at the scaly landscape that had inspired such an afternoon of rich regression.

For a long moment, I held my breath. Nothing looked as it should have – the dragon tail feature nowhere to be seen. Fog was tearing across the space where I had expected to see it. Barely ten minutes had passed and the landscape was unrecognisable. Disorientated, I started to retrace my steps. White wisps raced eerily across the slope, revealing unfriendly patches of rock before swallowing them up again.

In one of those clearances, as I frantically scanned the slope for a way down it, the tail re-emerged. It was hard to take in the shock of its location. Somehow I had overshot it and dropped at an angle, ending up the wrong side of it. Not only that, the distance of my descent was further than seemed possible. The spine of rock was at least a hundred feet higher up than me. Cliffs with deadly falls lay in between, which I would meet if I continued to cut across. I felt a rising panic. There were only two hours left before it got dark. I had to move quickly and decisively. At least I now knew how dangerously I had veered off course.

I scrambled up, feeling the surge of energy and focus that comes from fear. Only once I was considerably above the dragon tail, I allowed myself to drop to the other side, hoping the goat's trail that had brought me there would flash into view. I headed for a dense patch of scrub and ploughed through it, ignoring the bristling scrapes through my drenched trousers. The gnarly stumps were useful handrails and footholds to stop me from slipping, as I quickened my pace.

That went on longer than was comfortable. At last free of it, my spirits soared as the faint trail appeared again among some rocks that looked familiar. The terrain had become friendlier and greener. A grassy area opened up with an oak tree, bending towards the valley that I'd noticed on the way up. A flat smooth seat on which to rest had been fashioned by three perfectly assembled rocks, as if someone had put them there for an occasion such as this to draw breath. It was a perfect armchair with an outstanding view on a clear day. The pressure was over. I knew the way down, achievable by dark.

Sitting on the slabs, I delved into my pockets for some gloves. As well as a coin, there was a perfectly twisted cone of a shell, that I had forgotten about since finding it on a beach some months back. All of a sudden, it felt right to plant it right there, beneath the oak and next to a young sapling sprung from it. Helpfully, a small rock was nestled between them that had gouged a perfect nook for the shell. Underneath it was a surprise: an identical shell in shape and twist to my own, only miniature, nestled in the moist soil. It had the same pearly sheen and sharp end, pointing to a spiral's unending trajectory. In a miracle of chance, there had been an old shell in my coat – and I had somehow stumbled across the perfect resting space for it: alongside its Bugarach sister. It had found its buried twin. What a sweet moment; how suddenly life could change! The disorientating muddle within the spiral had led to this timely reminder that not everything was as it seemed. A design could exist within chaos, no matter how unlikely. Like the eclipse that day – and finding out about how important it was in ancient Egypt. When I starved myself of mystery, I suffered. How hollow a day could seem as a stream of disconnected events and encounters; all the lonelier for being empty of sentiment or meaning.

Didn't this shell matching up with another lift for a moment the solitary endurance, as I often experienced it, of being human? It inspired in me the same wonder felt elsewhere, linking other times and places. For there was an echo of this synchronicity only striking me now. It was some years before, one afternoon outside Cologne's celebrated cathedral. On a dirty pavement square, my eye had been drawn to a bit of scuffed litter, a four-pointed paper star, folded as origami. I'll never know why but I had picked it up. On it, someone had written "ha, ha, ha". Without a thought, I put it in my pocket, not questioning the curious impulse to do that. Later, about to throw it away, I had unfolded it to see how it had been made. Inside, the neatest handwriting and words:

I walk alone I walk a…
I walk this empty street
On the Boulevard of Broken Dreams Where the city sleeps,
And I'm the only one and I walk a…
My shadow's the only one that walks beside me,
My shallow heart's the only one that's beating
Sometimes, I wish someone out there will find me, Till then I walk alone…

Whoever had penned those lyrics had touched something in me. I later found out they were from a song by the American punk band Green Day. What mattered was the sentiment they captured for a stranger, another soul recognising their lonely shadow. What sweetness in alliances forged in darker moments.

And yet there on Bugarach I hadn't felt really alone: benevolence had accompanied my every step of that long day – also my inseparable shadow. There had been a bigger orchestration, the spiral guiding me to witness the charged content of my history. Those memories were still alive, carrying the same energy as I had originally experienced them. Unresolved feelings – regret, sadness, bitterness and anger – lived on in a tandem otherworld, preying on the joy that was innately mine. My journey was to transform them. I was being urged to go deeper still, through the doorways I had seen lined up – each one a gateway to another vivid chapter in my life. What I knew now was that some things could only be discovered through being felt. The shell had reminded me that no matter how things could look, I was never really alone.

Back at the empty gîte, as I fumbled with keys at the bedroom door, the neighbouring one opened: it was Patrick. At a glance, he looked as rough as if he had been blown about the mountain all day as I had been. He lit up, apparently delighted to see me again and was eager to share all that had happened since we met. There were photos to show me, stories to tell of strange people inhabiting this mysterious area; theories and counter theories of alien inhabitants – of black magic practices and sects with impenetrable hierarchies, guarding secrets to unofficial human histories, lethal knowledge only for initiates.

In the rather seedy light, the rings round Patrick's eyes looked all the darker as he briefed me about one "crazy" person he had met after another. He offered me a roll-up and we headed outside. It was raining very gently and stars could be seen through patchy cloud billowing across the valley. The storm I had seen on the horizon up at Bugarach hadn't passed over.

"How exhausting this trip has been!" I exclaimed to Patrick, as I spotted Orion's Belt. It was one of the most hallowed constellations in ancient Egypt for being the home of Lord Osiris, Lord of the Underworld – the gateway to the realms of the afterlife.

"Bugarach is really *magnétique*," he concluded, blowing out some smoke. "What am I doing here, man?" he asked of the sky.

"Yes," I replied, "what are we doing here?"

For a moment, I felt so glad of Patrick's fleeting company – Patrick, who mirrored my own blind stumble through a time of vibrant world change. Like countless seekers before us, we had coincided out of a hunch that something worth discovering lay just around the next corner or rise. That was all there ever was to go on, a lunge at peace, open to the mystery – in declaring a purpose for the bafflingly beautiful and still so challenging business, known as 'life'.

"Hey I've got to tell you about Mary Magdalene and her story here, man," Patrick piped up, putting the butt of his cigarette in his pocket, as I took one last puff, noticing Orion had vanished.

But that really would be another story, from another time and portal within the spiral that had opened up so graphically on the cliff at Bugarach – over the chasm, the vast space that could swallow all the stories living within me whole.

Chapter 7

Jungle Medicine

Time, unlike a river, is said to flow in both directions. Events upstream and those downstream course along the Here and Now of the Present, a harbour for all destinations, past and future. Nowhere is ever fixed. Where there are witnesses, there are as many landscapes. Perception shifts what there is to see; hindsight or projection also casting their shadows over what is really present. My story, as I frame it, can spring alive with a backward glance, brightening and darkening in different ways from how it was lived at the time. With the perspective that time brings, with wings to survey, I understand a far greater narrative unfolding through me as I then stumbled within labyrinths of crushing darkness towards a pinprick of light.

Some four years before Mount Bugarach loomed in my own life's trajectory, I heard the Amazon whispering to me – like an unmistakable rush of distant water. The jungle could be felt many thousands of miles away, a whole ocean between us. It shimmered in my dreams and took life in my imagination as a mysterious entity, vital and intelligent. Its intensity became a coax, taunting me as the unrest that had always been there. It was only a matter of time before I would visit, for the river's calling, I now know, was a summons, beckoned by her, the guardian of the psyche's deepest depths. Like the urgent call of the 'Upside Down Mountain', the feverish pull to the jungle, it was to turn out, was her summoning me all over again. Only I didn't know that at the time. I was only aware that I had to visit the Amazon.

Known in some tribal tales as the womb of the planet, the river's irrepressible power is as much about the mulch of death as the life it generates. As certain plants and medicines in Amazon lore are affectionately coined 'mother' for their nurturing qualities, I was to adopt my own nickname for the mother of them all: Grandmother – the mother of all mothers, all such intelligent life forms, green or blue, and every colour in between. Grandmother is as familiar and intimate as she is elusive and impersonal. It is an exacting relationship: she demands death for the fullness of life to express. This is what I was to understand much later as her invitation: to make the journey of descent 'consciously' this time round. Raking over the ins and outs of past drama, trawling through many mind-expanding or heart-opening moments, is not my intention. Allowing feelings not fully expressed their light of day is the only reason to voyage deeper into memory. Awareness was the first step, feeling through a doorway of buried emotion the next. Venturing downstream, back to the Amazon, is a choice to relive the darkness that swamped me there – and feel it transform.

I bought my first ticket to the jungle two weeks after a friend had enthused about a life-changing experience there. She had taken part in a shamanic ceremony in which the psychotropic brew ayahuasca was served. The vine, held as sacred in Amazonian culture, has transformative powers known to illumine the most buried depths of the psyche. It was regarded as the ultimate mind and heart-expanding medicine, offering in the main an unforgiving dose of no-nonsense wisdom. As a psychedelic escape, caution was required: demons and dragons, angels and deities could also hop aboard for the trip. Ayahuasca, most agreed, stoked up hidden turmoil a seeker might not want to confront.

Hearing about the brew's excavating nature attracted me at once. It sounded like a piercing ally for self-inquiry. Generally I was grateful for many things: good health and friends, managing a time-rich, cash-poor balance that had not strayed into debt. There were always short-term jobs to pick up here and there, including freelance writing. Still, a tension lurked behind my gratitude. I didn't swallow the positive hard line of New Age thinking and its investment in happy outcome – the resolve to 'grin and bear it', or 'smile and keep smiling until you can bear it'. I knew how perception changed the world, but denying the grit giving rise to less desirable feelings as unworthy to the cause of 'one day enlightenment' at least fired up the very irritation I was supposed to have meditated out of myself. Whatever I had tried or denied, nothing was ever enough, other than a simmering impatience that rarely exhausted itself. The fact was no manner of good friends and fortune, of 'growing' prospects, and no amount of self-improvement events and books could ever quite hammer out of me a sense of leased peace. The twinge, as I have called it, might subside for days, weeks, and often months at a time. But it would be back. When I heard of ayahuasca for the first time, I only knew then that imagining the Amazon and its plant medicines quickened something in me – an excitement to change my life story, and to live that change.

My travels began downstream in Iquitos, the biggest city in the Peruvian jungle. The sultry climate promised all the sensuousness and charge of fatal attraction. Iquitos was a chaos of modern and traditional forces, a sprawl of faded colonial charm. It had sprung from rubber trade more than a century before, thriving as the main world supplier until competition opened up, plunging the boomtown into oblivion. Rapid expansion had since destroyed tradition: auto-rickshaws and scooters overrunning the narrow boat and canoe. Oil, tourism, research and charitable social infrastructure were the lifeblood of Iquitos. Encroaching the city, the jungle's natural contrasts were unending; bursts of colour among sullen, earthy hues, dragonflies and butterflies of every pattern and size, flocks of squawking birds commuting over the canopy beyond each morning, returning at dusk. Being close to the equator, day and night swung equally, twelve hours apart. Within extremes so evident lay an exacting balance.

Iquitos also carried the distinction of being the launch pad for seekers of ayahuasca, like myself. On that first two-week visit to the Earth's largest garden, I discovered a vivid snapshot of nature and her laws. Ayahuasca itself was not only a portal to subtle realms beyond sensory reach; it was an invitation to embrace the whole of life, in all its unseen possibility. Such psychic recesses were usually only accessed by shamans, master voyagers of worlds and everything in between. Ingesting ayahuasca opened those spaces for everyone else.

I had found a shamanic centre a short drive outside Iquitos that had two head shamans, or Maestros. To be qualified for that title of mastery demanded years of immersing with the plants, and practising their medicine. One was a *nativo*, the other an American, one of the few Western Ayahuasceros with enough experience to hold ceremonies for large groups. There were enough stories on the grapevine of predatory, power-crazed shamans or incompetent ones, preying on the wallet or vulnerability of naive gringos. Some would emerge from the jungle lost, and in much worse shape than when they had arrived. The set-up I chose had a reputation for combining tradition with the reassuringly familiar language of Western psychology. Such a combination inspired my confidence, offering a steady bridge into the uncharted territory of an opened psyche. It felt safe. It meant I could dive into the unknown feeling fully supported.

In darkness, the shamans sang hauntingly melodic songs called 'icaros'. They were like sonic wings guiding a ceremony's flight through the labyrinthine worlds of ayahuasca. Sung in Spanish, English, different jungle dialects and also a 'plant language', playful and sweet, they often inspired elevated insights and wisdom. As the energy within the ceremony built, so did the visionary effect of the medicine, known as 'mareacion'. The brew's gifts were often presented with sweet tenderness, other times as a glaring spotlight on hidden truths. Such a rich mix was an expression of the vine's vibrant home, where the epic drama of survival and death played out vividly; predator and prey battling on a stage of growth and decay.

Similarly, ayahuasca could open up delicately interconnecting realms of intense vitality or barrenness within my vision. Life and consciousness, as it showed me, were one and the same thing.

Ceremonies were demanding physically too. Ayahuasca was a purgative. True to its prehensile form, it could probe and extract from deep within the body anything ripe to be expelled. Tension and nausea escalated until they were purged – through sweating, yawning, shaking, laughing and crying, vomiting and defecation. The physical release of dense energetic forms could be gruelling, as layer upon layer of personal history were shed.

In that first taste of the jungle, it was evident how shamanic practices and their potential for healing probed far beyond the symptoms treated by clinical cures and formulas. Illness was seen as soul sickness, imbalance manifesting from within the matrix of relationships – among people and families, their environment, diet and society. In traditional medicine, disease was as much a state of the spirit as it was the body. To fix an ill body without addressing what made it that way only suppressed its real causes. Like the jungle's complex web of relationships, human dynamics were just as interwoven with forces either nurturing or destructive to one's well-being. Ignored over time, they could attack with cancerous intent.

Ayahuasca tourism was beginning to boom: more and more Westerners seeking holistic treatment for their mental and physical health. The shamans warned those of us preparing to return home that materialism carried a price: divorcing from the true source of food, shelter and clothes killed the spirit of community. We had forgotten where we came from. And it was true, feeling refreshed after an immersion in such pure verdant space, I started to remember the glare of electric skylines and urban stresses from which I had relished my escape.

Settling back into my routine in England, I knew I'd only scratched the surface of the medicine's dimension – and my whole being yearned to explore more deeply. The opaque world of cause and effect was fascinatingly interwoven. Nothing happened in isolation. Exploring what lay behind a symptom could open up a warren of twisting trails. No matter how disease might manifest – physically, mentally or emotionally – there was a similar root: wounded self-relationship. It reminded me of the fairy tale *The Princess and the Pea* – no amount of mattresses could flatten the pea at the bottom of the heap.

I read everything I could about core shamanic practices, and began an intensive eighteen-month training in energy healing rooted in the Andean tradition of Peru. I learnt how to journey into altered states of consciousness, using the sound of a rattle or drumbeat as guides. My senses became more attuned to the invisible world of energy and how to map it. Before long, I was able to deepen and practise the discoveries I had made for myself drinking ayahuasca – and the underlying relationships sabotaging a healthy mind and body. Sometimes the link wasn't so obvious. I wanted to understand more about the origin of disease, to support others to explore the source of their own anxiety however that might physically play out. New discoveries were also being made each week in the Amazon among the cornucopia of barks and leaves. The healing arts were an unlimited science – and I was eager to learn whatever I could. A psychotropic medicine to open up the more impenetrable layers of the mind, and its relationship to the body, kept calling me to return, as clearly as a broadcast invitation.

Ten months after that first experience with ayahuasca, I was back in the jungle for a stay of two months. Three months after that, I moved there. Like the snap of an elastic band, my enthusiasm would face a prolonged engagement with a teacher of equal intensity. My life's direction, it then seemed, was a one-way ticket to the Amazon, to explore its inexhaustible medicine bag.

Chapter 8

Warriorship

I had arrived in Iquitos, that third time, with a rucksack and plenty of spiritual ambition. The plan was to learn from the shamans where I had been a client. In an exchange of emails, I'd expressed my passionate curiosity for their tradition, and it was agreed, in return for this immersion, I would help out and share my own background in shamanic practices. There were similarities and core differences that could support the powerful transformative potential of ayahuasca, which required years of disciplined training to master. Before I had even started as a novice assistant, the no-nonsense practicalities of a do-or-die shamanic culture was laid bare – in my first dressing down from the Maestro who owned the centre.

The first three weeks had dragged as I waited to be welcomed to Iquitos by the head shaman who was ill in bed. I practised my Spanish, visited remoter jungle villages by boat, and loitered around the cafés and diners meeting an assortment of locals and gringos. My first official day at work was looming, with the arrival of thirty or so clients, and I was eager to be briefed as to what would be expected of me. In the agreement forged before heading out to Peru, I was to have my own clients and hold private sessions with them all morning. In the afternoons, I would lead group meditations or guided journeys to help integrate the effects of the medicine. At night, I would help out as instructed in the next ceremony.

One afternoon, I bumped into a friend who had seen the Maestro in town, apparently on form again. Expecting to hear from him, three days passed and still there had been no contact. I wrote a rather hasty email – how glad I was to hear he was better, and disappointed not to have seen him yet, having moved to Peru to work for him, after all. There were just two or three days left to meet up before my job began, I had pointed out.

The Maestro – I was unlikely to forget again – was not someone to confront. His emailed reply made it clear that role was for him to initiate, and without dialogue. Rule number one, I had to follow the strict directive of his leadership. There was a hierarchy in system for vital reasons – a militaristic ranking structure with corresponding titles to advance in the medicine. I would work my way up from the very bottom, through the demonstration of my skill and experience. Answering him back, or showing him disrespect as I had done, could cost me my life in that shamanic universe in which he'd cut some muscle.

My spirits for a moment plunged. Rereading the email, there was no ambiguity or shade of humour. I would have to be more careful: my status evidently very different from the fee-paying client I had been – more like wayward underling. At least, I consoled myself, my impetuousness had elicited some clarity: a new identity of sorts. I was to take a place on the lowest rung conceived for me, as 'intern'. Above it were, in Spanish, the levels of Captain, Major and Commander, issued to an apprentice only after a relentless demonstration of diligence and commitment. This lineage reinforced the need for safety such a strict system supported – the challenges evident managing large groups and their chaotic, often overpowering energies.

Amazonian shamanism, at the level I entered it, was like being dumped by a bus downtown in a strange city at the dead of night. The apprentices who'd been there for some years were a tight circle and welcomed me cautiously, with friendly cool. They were used to the rigorous demands of their practice and limited free time. Mixing with them, I got used to the language of protection and defence, as well as a street wisdom extending to other realities within the spirit realms. We were continually alert to the potentially fatal dangers of inter-lineage jealousy and power play among shamans. Incredible stories of astral battles and psychic theft were staple. Witchcraft and superstition were an everyday matter in the native community. Hiring someone to do wrong to another through energetic manipulation and intent was as routine as rainstorms. The threats were real: defence strategies were a core part of an apprentice's training for the daily sorcery they faced; even one Maestro, with forty years experience, fell to the floor during a ceremony, needing help to remove the psychic arsenal embedded in him. A sucking technique, known as extraction, posed a real danger to the other shaman assisting, who also risked ingesting it. We had all watched on silently as the Maestro groaned faintly throughout the procedure. The shaman began to suck over his colleague's thigh where he had been hurt, making a series of loud slurping sounds as the witchcraft was extracted. Every few seconds, he would then spit it out. Whatever had been there – invisible to ordinary eyes – made an audible 'pop' as it landed in the bucket.

For a Westerner used to independent travel to far-flung places but fresh green within other realities, this culture was going to take time to get used to. Understanding what lay beneath my self-driven impulses would, in time, demand a very gritty initiation. The schedule, as a novice, was not undemanding. The tours were nine-days long with a week's gap between. Thirty guests were a typical average, and each time, new names, personalities and their chemistry would play into a lively energetic mix. To be immersed with vibrant explorers of mystical ideas and other realms was a privilege. At times, it was hard to imagine a more wonderful way to live. It also meant there was little distraction or every day anchor to ease the all-consuming nature of life in camp. Exhaustion felt normal – the routine was too structured to give in to tiredness. Until returning to the restorative comforts of Iquitos, I would wander about, content and dreamy; the fatigue fuelling a continually altered state while in the jungle.

A ceremony itself could last four hours, experienced as infinite. Clock time lost all meaning. I would be working through my own process, having also drunk ayahuasca, and support anyone as required. Afterwards, throughout the night if necessary, I was on hand for those still steeped in the *mareacion*, which could go on well into the next day. That was true for me too. I was lucky if I had four hours sleep before the routine started up again. From breakfast until lunch, I offered intensive private sessions with guests. The hut I worked from was a haven tucked away from the main jungle campus. Those moments between seeing people were my chance to rebalance and ground for the continuing ride.

The work was always demanding and varied. Most of the time I loved it. Exorcisms, demonic confrontations, aura cleansing and chakra balancing, illuminations and extractions were all in a day's schedule. In the dreamy lull of late afternoon, using a drum or rattle, I'd hold guided journeys for healing, perspective and rejuvenation. After that, I would need to prepare the ceremonial hut for the repeat adventure.

As well as ayahuasca, we worked with many other plants, tree barks and roots. The shamanic 'dieta' was a critical part of our training. At its most literal, over a number of days (diets can last months) we would drink a mix of barks fermenting in water. Their energetic properties were activated by the shaman's *icaro*. By drinking them, their spirits enter the body, transferring their qualities into one's awareness and constitution. During the diet and afterwards, the tree takes life, instructing its host as a resident teacher. The greatest learning and cleansing happened with those *dietas* – involving a deeper mental excavation and intensity of focus. But they demanded strict discipline. We could only eat the blandest food, freshwater fish, plantains and a sludgy tasteless manioc drink. The key abstentions were no salt, sugar, caffeine or alcohol and no soap, cream, toothpaste or medication of any kind. There could be no sex either – to breach this could have very uncomfortable consequences. Energetically, the medicines were opening us up and the science of that was exacting. Those of us working at the centre dieted alongside the clients we looked after. Everything, all interaction with others and the inanimate world, was an exchange of energy. We had to be guarded to keep strong for the work, and to allow the medicines of the trees to grow within our energetic bodies.

In that climate and with all the purging, the lack of salt for the nine-day *dieta* was debilitating. By the end of it, just walking a short distance took resolve. The sweltering humidity could weigh upon any urge to do anything but swing in a hammock. The other restrictions had a more subtle impact: in particular the no-sex rule. Appropriately, the centre had a strict policy of no intimacy with guests or among staff. In truth none of us could have been open to any intimate relationship with the diets' continuing abstentions. My seniors spoke of "clean" energy – and regarded celibacy as the best way to maintain shamanic impeccability. Compared to horror stories of predatory shamans elsewhere, and female clients seduced by the glamour of their powerful Maestro, where I worked was, to use their benchmark, 'clean'. Officially, the set-up was impeccable.

The sexual energy was still at times intoxicating, intensified by the strict rules. As boundaries were upheld in words and actions, a shadowy unacknowledged realm coexisted. Ceremonies were often unforgiving as the medicine amplified shady distortions mirroring back in grim parody. Ambiguity, projections, reflections, assumptions and outright fairy tales were all too believable in the fever of the jungle – a bacchanalian other-world alongside the strict management, in which I too colluded. It was a seductive mix. The environment resembled a boy's-own club. The prevailing sense of humour was edgy and outright crude. The values of "warriorship" were modelled for fighting in the astral worlds of rough and tumble. Male shamans in the Amazon greatly outnumbered women. It was often implied women could be more vulnerable and less suited to the clear-cut principles of psychic defence. The distinction creeped into the cultural language and I was wary of being thrown in with that generality. One unfortunate night, I unwittingly created for myself the shaft down which I would tumble for months to come.

The head shaman was a trailblazer, an outsider to the jungle, who barely out of college was drawn to the Amazon and never left. Like hundreds of other clients before me, he commanded my absolute trust and respect. The Maestro was tall and handsome (a statement made by men and women alike), charming and witty (he could make a crowd laugh until it hurt), with a charismatic irreverence for anyone else's opinion. His stories were entertaining and extraordinary, making Carlos Castaneda's cult tales of Yaqui sorcery seem outdated. He was also not only a bachelor but strictly celibate. The more boundaried his resistance, the more magnetic he became, his personality spilling out as a brilliant wit. He managed a twist of self-deprecation too, which certainly did not extend to his style of leadership. The Maestro made little secret of having to deal with female clients who were convinced they'd crack his bachelor's status. To my personal regret, I too, for what seemed like long weeks, believed I was at the front of that queue. During one intense night in ceremony of achingly lurid visions, I declared my feelings. The next day the number two in command – whose title was Mayor in Spanish – Major – passed on the official response from the top: sort myself out or leave.

Politics are just as prevalent in spiritual circles as anywhere else. The talented shamans I worked with and admired expected appropriate respect and recognition. Time and again, I fell short of those tacit boundaries. One day I overheard the Maestro telling guests how tips were shared equally between all his staff. Later, choosing my moment carefully, no one else around, I pointed out as meekly as I could how those tips had never reached me. As 'intern', I added, I also paid for my board. There was an awkward pause, so rare for someone ready with opinion.

Quickly he recovered, a flush of red the only giveaway he had been made uncomfortable. He would get back to me on this – and never did.

Some weeks later, I experienced the familiar flutter of fear as another message was dispatched to me via the Mayor. The Maestro, he reported, did not appreciate my lack of respect generally – citing various examples of where I had unconsciously slipped up, either in my work or general demeanour about camp. Again, I wrestled with plunging spirits; no matter how much I tried to meet the Maestro's exacting expectations, my status seemed sealed as dubious. However hard I tried to rein myself in, or apply myself to my clients and medicine work, the glaring truth couldn't be ignored any longer: I simply didn't fit in. But surely, I reasoned, fretting again and again over the Maestro's indifference to me, my point about tips shouldn't have been kept back. Only, no matter how much I tried to reassure myself, I couldn't quite summon the trust to know the difference between integrity and tactlessness.

However lost and lonely I felt, I wasn't miserable enough to let go of the dream to become a shamanic healer, a Curandera, in which I was so invested. The Amazon's unique vitality continually renewed and distracted my flagging spirits. The taste of machismo was wrapped in the jungle's mesmerising beauty, which seeped through the barriers of fragile egos and their tension. Even all things solid such as homes and buildings had to be fortified against its mulching procession. Plants of every fragrance and colour flourished in the damp heat, inspiring the heart and mind with similar persistence. I could feel my body awake to the musicality of nature, its beats and rhythms, the same hip-centric swagger in how locals walked, taking life in me; all the time in the world for wandering or hanging out. Between tours, I relished the freedom – which slipped away too quickly. Dancing was natural to old and young alike. A foot might tap and fingers click, a bottom jut and shake sassily at the faintest bass.

Yet the pace was slow, always time for a nap and a strut going nowhere in particular. Rain and storms would clear the air of languor and tension – and the pulse would start up all over again, as sure as a drumbeat. So, I continued on, determined to ignore the strains within and around me.

Looking far downstream, at my life then in the jungle, I can now see Grandmother biding her time, watching me thrash about in a nightmare from which I couldn't wake up. Only then I didn't know her, not yet aware of her guardianship. One evening, just before a ceremony, she tried to wake me up: as a tarantula – charging me among a throng of people. It was as if the tarantula had spotted me from the other side of the hut, scuttling across metres of space until it paused at my feet, ignoring everyone else. My screams alerted a cook to rush to my aid with a broom. It felt disturbingly personal, as if I'd been singled out; not the other way round – that it was Grandmother in disguise, summoned by me! She also visited me one night in a dream as a plague of spidery crabs. In the dream, I was driving along a glistening ocean under a full moon, when thousands as one pincered mass scrabbled up from the beach and swamped the ruts left by my car. At Mount Bugarach I was to discover how Grandmother transforms whatever lurks unseen in the labyrinths of the mind. It is only now, way upstream, that I can recognise her among the jungle shadows, as I lurched on through my internship.

Six months into it and something was beginning to harden in me. I was deeply insecure but no longer as fascinated by the Maestro in whom I had placed all my trust. After the debacle over tips, no matter how hard I tried to fit in, the more I exacerbated the delicate status quo. There was now no opportunity for direct contact, never being admitted into his hallowed circle, which gathered around him, poring over his every word and quip. He had isolated me, relaying any messages by Mayor as necessary. It was only a matter of time before something in me was going to snap.

I yearned to be recognised by the senior shamans I admired. No criticism meant I was on track: silence from the top was a positive thumbs-up. In ceremonies I wasn't allowed to sing, despite songs inspired by the medicine rising within me: I wasn't ready, they said – my energy needed more cleansing. I pretended I didn't mind, and swallowed my sadness – wrestling with jealousy at the melodious voices of the other apprentices driving each ceremony forwards. The frustration I also felt was compounded by all the talk espousing universality: oneness, love and the rest. So at odds with my everyday experience, my loneliness and sense of exclusion seemed all the more acute. I lost myself in my work and friendships with guests, but could never share how troubled I continually felt.

The jungle began closing in. It was a place without horizon – a setting or rising sun only imagined. Such suffocating containment only intensified the bliss and horror unfolding. Sometimes my throat felt strangled. Perhaps the shamans were right – I needed to clean up. They could see more than me – they had more experience, more insight. I couldn't risk trusting a hint of rebellion nudging me gently to speak out, to step forwards. I had exchanged perhaps no more than an hour's conversation with the Maestro in six months since my confessionary meltdown that ceremony early on in my internship. Communication was limited to orders, criticism or the perfunctory feedback of thank you. Once when a group of clients enthused about the results they were experiencing with me, number two was dispatched to warn me: stop sending those sycophants to him.

El Maestro's afternoon lectures began to infuriate me – holding court for hours at a time, to an enthralled audience. Behind the scenes, I had heard him mocking some of his more ardent admirers. Was anyone actually listening – really following his declarations of reality and how the universe worked? Over time, the talks sounded to my ears like rants – verbose and emphatic. For someone who could state so simply that love was universal intelligence, his understanding of its more mysterious laws was a great deal more laboured. There had been a time when nothing could seem more entertaining than being guided by him through vast realms of existential science day after day. This teacher, dazzling and original, knew so much more than anyone else did. His opinions and digressions were never ambivalent. Such certainty had answered my every question. As I began to mistrust his knowledge and unshakable confidence, I felt all the lonelier for having no one in whom I could confide my growing doubts. Seeing through him was an admission of my own poor judgment. After all, my blind admiration had amounted to giving my power away – could I really trust my own ability to discern?

Meanwhile, the ceremonies escalated in intensity, no matter how small my dose. The visions could plunge from angelic to apocalyptic, and outright demonic. I purged buckets of shame and horror as l confronted a conveyor belt of manifestations peering out from behind their enclosure, a Rocky Horror show of extremes: Queen of the ice, the little Miss Princess, power-crazed witch, pervert and liar, the muted fool. Different stages of my personal history rose from the depths of my being, shunted back from decades of suppression. Every lie and unkind word, every arrogant assumption and outright cruelty was there to be seen as family and friends, acquaintances, lovers and boyfriends paraded through my awareness. Every one had played their part in a chain of disempowerment I had created. The men in particular were set up to crash from pedestals as fallen heroes and villains, or embody the star quality of untouchable talent, with a few duller roles in between – and these dysfunctional projections and relationships extended outside ceremony. The shamans I admired and mistrusted were simply part of that unending story.

I chose to stay – not yet ready to admit the extent of my

loneliness – that my dream had collapsed. Leaving the jungle was not an option. The work was cut out for me. It was limitless – after all a hook will always catch something if left to dangle. As Grandmother would later tell me, you marry or divorce what you don't own as yours. I had traded one set of challenging dramatis personae for another. But I was ensnared. Perception, I was discovering, was seeing whatever you were ready and willing to see. Like the butterfly fluttering along with gentle persistence given its short life of flight, I too brushed against beauty and pain, sadness as well as incredible kinship; friendships and connections forged for a lifetime within a fragile dichotomy of love and fear. All along, the prevailing teaching of love haunted me, mocked by all evidence to the contrary. My dream of finding an enduring vocation, a purpose to give my life direction, was in tatters, my self-belief shattered. After many months of fighting against the current, ignoring the daily clues to quit, I was close to being consumed by the biggest danger of all: despair.

Chapter 9

Dethroning

One starry evening, beneath the exquisite constellations of the southern hemisphere, the earth spongy beneath my feet, I intended to move through the deadlock. I couldn't stay on at the centre – the feeling of inadequacy and not fitting in was unbearable. And I couldn't see anything beyond it either: where to go next or what to do. The ceremony was minutes away, and there was a palpable tension around camp in the countdown.

A sliver of crescent moon hung low in the sky, beside two bold stars twinkling in dialogue. A breeze swept through the jungle like a sigh. Thick trees near the ceremonial hut towered in the dark like anthropomorphic giants, their bushy leaves mops of sprouting hair. I could feel a soothing presence spilling out from the encroaching canopy. For all the fever of sound and life, there was a quality of poise that evening, even in the faintest rustle and barely perceptible breeze. I imagined this presence as aware of me as I was it – a magnificent maternal being, with all the patience to lie in wait, until the every particle birthed from her had been reclaimed.

Settling down inside with everyone else, I silently invoked ayahuasca's help, as I gulped back the bitter brew and waited. Quickly, the meditative whoosh of the *chakapas*, their fan of air following the rhythm of opening *icaros*, brought on the *mareacion*. The sounds from outside animated in my visions. A gentle start was never reassuring for long: after beautiful preambles into the benevolence of the cosmos, the medicine at last picked me up within a giant wave and crashed me into the open hand of a force that had been biding its time.

An unmistakable roar of a puma pulled my awareness out of the hut into deep jungle. I was at the mercy of impenetrable darkness. In the foreboding, my tension caught alight, encircling me in fire. The flames were low and unsettled, in them a tribe of people hunched together; old and young, babies heaped within their mothers' arms. Staring out from haunted eyes, they looked as desperate as animals cornered, unable to escape the horror they faced.

Those people merged with other scenes of devastation: a parched wasteland with wisps of charred grass; swarming flies sensing death. Toxicity seeped from the gnarled roots of trees no longer embedded in the earth. Carcasses of animals littered the land. Nothing could live there. The picture switched: lush forest was now swamp. The bitter irreversibility of destruction could be felt. Maggots filled rotting stumps and dead birds. The air was thick with mosquitos and the stench of death. This once exotic garden was the drab hue of decay, as the bones of emaciated scavenging animals seemed to rattle in the unnatural quiet. Lifelessness had a quality of sound. The stark finality of ravage was not the natural order. This was a snapshot of imbalance, of nature turning against itself. Waters began flooding the space of disease, an irrepressible force. The tribe had felt the very menace now gripping me; their brothers and sisters everywhere threatened.

The fire was not finished. A crone, scrunched and lined as dried mud, stared out from black hollowed eyes. The force of death in her expressed as cold laughter. "You… You!" she cried, her voice scratchy and shrill. Her forefinger prodded the air. "You choose! To stray from your nature is to destroy it!" She was then gone but her warning lingered. Straying from balance bred disease – the land would exact a terrible cost. Life unleashed rage at such sacrilege.

I was too exhausted to fight my fear. It had come to this. Finally I had awoken to my true nature. An apocalypse was playing out everywhere I could see – in my world and in me. It was inevitable. I was within the clutch of Hell – with all the pain and torment of loneliness. I knew the desperation of believing myself as separate from everything else. I also understood the gift in that – without the force that divides, life couldn't happen. No narrative, no me or you, no this in relation to that. Nothingness itself. As sure as the world of form divided, it could also unite. That very satanic essence enabled the colour red to be beheld among other shades, without which redness couldn't exist. I understood the necessity for everything to have its place – including the heartbreaking spectrum of human experience that could seem so loveless and sad.

No such insight, however reasonable, could shake off the certainty I was damned. I felt swallowed by the weight of wretchedness. Somewhere from within the abyss over which I teetered, a malign force was pressing on me to surrender. It wanted me to give up to it, the home where I really belonged: into the black nothingness, alone and forgotten. Talons gripped me as in a vice and hurled me into the black space – my every cell dense with nausea, tension strangling every breath, unease throbbing within every muscle and tissue.

The purge was unrelenting. Choking with vomit, I stumbled through the darkness and crashed into the 'baño'. In the dark, slumped on a toilet, time stopped. Eyes open or closed, there was no let up in the purgatory where I found myself, robbed of any instinct for hope. Exhausted, there was nothing left in me to fight. It was easier to give up, to bargain with the force, a nulli-fying entity, that could give me a stab at peace, until the next time. There was nothing but darkness, so what difference would it make to give myself over fully to it?

I plummeted. This was a nightmare impossible to wake up from. Dimly, screams and shrieks of others in their own ugly wasteland of extremes arose in my awareness. I had no will left to even sigh. Hours must have passed as I remained there, limp and empty. I finally knew who I was – the daughter of darkness, a lonely soul, hounded by every other hungry ghost. I was forever lost, unaccounted for. My loveless life was not my own. The numbness was eternal. The ghostly whisper of the *chakapa* had become a roar. The distinctive voice of a native Maestro shaman merged with the whole of my being. It was a sound not at all human. Neither was it external to me. Each tone was strange and otherworldly, emanating from within me as serpents and pyramids of moving colour. Every word of his powerful *icaro* conjured a vivid world of sonic colour.

> Cielo Cielo Ayahuascacitoini,
> Troncoimanacitoine Papa Tuacitoini
> Ayudangichoini curangichoini cuerpocitoini
> Enderesangichioni sentiditoini Enderesangichioni sentiditoini
> Tranchilito sentiditoini no turbechiwongichoini
> Cushi cushi wayra wayra cuerpocitoini
> Todo todo mal espiritocitoini que venga contra de nostroscitoini chaparingi chapamongi
> Dragon rojo mama aguilitaini...

Shimmering labyrinths of breathtaking beauty as delicate as moth wings weave around me, oppressive and unending. A choking nausea has gripped my throat. I cough. I retch, gasping for air. Trapped!

There is a fault line running along my abdomen to my chest. An invisible scar, extending as far as my throat, coils around me. A pressure is gouging a fathomless hole deep in my gut. I have to remember to breathe. Breathe. Again, breathe. I let out the air quite deliberately but my shoulders are too knotted to loosen. I try again. They drop a little. I feel like the old wooden pump in the corner of my childhood home, the Priory. Among the faded orange bricks, beneath the trailing roses it looks handsome in its defunct way. A treasure to outlast time from when it was built. A Jacobean keepsake, with a squirt of oil in its thinning hinge, to move up and down. But there is no water left in the well it was

perches on her head, angular as a bent feather. A cloak drapes back revealing her narrow drooping shoulders. What looks like an unflattering effect of gravity over time is more than balanced by the horizontal sweep of her gaze suggested by her demeanour. She would have been the lady of the house. Staring out from the wall for posterity. A grandmother or mother-in-law – appeased by the cowering man who'd married into this slice of genteel Hampshire and the grandees who would have passed through. It was once a hunting lodge it is thought. Built for the debutantes escaping London and its smoky dirty streets – clean air among the forest would have then extended all the way to Surrey until Richmond. Oak was the lording tree of the thick wood surrounding the house. But what would those visiting city slickers have hunted, with lace ruffles and mannered whiskery beards and puffing clay pipes? Boar? Deer? With what – bows and arrows? This was pre-Guy Fawkes – pre-Gunpowder Plot. The tower at one end was to spot the Armada, they say. That can't be true if it was post Tudor. Did the arboreal viewing point offer the best vantage to spot prey for the hunt? And what then – motion to someone on horseback with hand signals pointing to the thick forest – 'that way'! So unlikely! Is that the best excitement in a slice of the 'olden days' historians can imagine? The gentlemen back then gambled in the small room at the bottom of the tower that became my bedroom. It's where I still sleep when I visit. The pipe smoke and particular smell of burning ash would have clouded the poky space very quickly.

Those old ghosts don't touch the seam running along my body. But I must persist – resurrecting the hidden life of the one place harbouring my deepest belonging. It was in this old building that I arrived into this world. So alive with the pulsing heart of history, surely it must know what lies disturbed, deep within the heart of the child born there, that was me? Twelve days after Winter Solstice – the shortest time of Winter before the long return to the sun – my birth was delivered in the Priory's largest room, named the Solar, a space for festivals and gatherings to share platters of harvest. The sunny heart of St Margaret's.

What of the seam now… is it opening a little? Does recalling the patch of land demarking my birth stir my entombment? I see a thorn from a flowerless tendril hovering over the shroud. If it pricks the corpse inside, ruby drops of blood would ooze. Would they drip down the taut skin, as veins of a decaying leaf? Where is the feeling in this captured hell? What is beneath the seam? Nothing, apparently. Not even numbness. That would suggest something without feeling to be there.

There is nothing there. That is my fear. I am afraid of being nothing, nothing to say, nothing to share, nothing to express, nothing to be, nowhere to go, a husk of something as nothing I suspect myself to be. Is that the fear, that in giving up all effort, all pretence at holding it together, nothing will hold it together and so I collapse, hollowed out? What has hollowed me out? Nothing I can recall. Nothing has happened – that really is the point. Nothing is happening. I have lost all direction and bearing. I am broken, but not really, as there is nothing needing to be mended. Something is cracking up in the nothing – a foundation, a floor smashing and breaking even though there's nothing there doing that. It's happening on its own, like a tremor deep inside it.

The Priory bricks, its features, its very character have withstood so much longer than my body. It's sacrilege, isn't it, to be this numb, so void of feeling that to behold its miracle and beauty is nothing but effort? It's trying, not being. It seems totally untruthful. Because that's not my impulse. My impulse is not to try, not to claim, not to declare or fashion and sculpt. I want to crack open and be cracked open, to behold a formless space and feel its wonder in just being that. I am feeling cramp again – a tightening of my muscles and limbs, my shoulders and neck. What is that – where does it come from?

Go deeper. Down! Feel more. Down deeper! Don't try. That's my mantra. That's the lifeline for the place of no shape, no name, where there really is no inclination to do anything but wait for the crushing, pointless emptiness to pass. I cannot wake up from this nightmare if that is what it is. I don't even need to crap out whatever lurks there, lumped and unmoving. No reason at all, just an endless crumpled sigh that I am, as I toss and turn, unable to root or enfold in it. What is it – what is holding me, as I tumble into another space, unable to make sense or shape of it and why I'm there. What am I doing there? Give up the effort of trying. Give in! Then what? What now? What is the fear of the nothing I am becoming – the blank page of no-thing – the scream with no impulse to be heard, as nothing expressing?

What to do, when I don't feel very much, stalled as I am in the comfortless refuge of my shallow thinking. Give me something – anything – please a theme, a movement – not this edgeless emptiness, with nothing to handrail me, nothing to surrender to. No words, form, people, story, no neat beginnings – because nothing has actually started, that is the point – all life arrested.

So, I am empty. Now what? There is nowhere to go – but dive into that emptiness.

Emptiness has a heavy heart – a pressure against the upper left rib cage. Emptiness sounds like the shrieks and moans of torment, the hum and whine of a persistent mosquito. Emptiness is the sink in front of me – which can wash my face when I have the energy, the will to get off this toilet seat. Emptiness is some hope, no matter how slight, of the ceremony ending, of this hideous visionary space dissolving, of my remembering that I really am loved. And I can love too. Emptiness is a cramping solar plexus. Emptiness is worry of the inertia that I have become. Emptiness is the projected depletion of my savings, and a resignation I never discovered a purpose or vehicle to travel through this endless time or break up the burden of my mind. Emptiness is the story I have wasted precious life. Emptiness is the fear I've got it wrong, I have nothing to share. I am nothing.

And now the thorn. What if it pricks the brow of the ashen white face that sleeps and is not really dead? Let's prick the throat visible among the folds of cloth. Let it bleed the heart, so a sigh can escape. A long one. Weary with the weight of unexplored emptiness. Focus on the feet – the soles of the feet, somehow peeping out at the bottom. Bloodletting. More of that, please, thorn. I feel an imbalance in the soles of my feet. Let me track a little more. The left feels unused, fresher in feel, less exercised. It is lighter than the right foot?

Feel! Feel what? There's nothing there.

Go deeper. I'm in a well. The space with murky water at the bottom reaching my ankles. I'm swallowed within a cylinder open at the top. Above is light and space. I sense the promise of a tree, as a breeze stirs through the jungle I know is really out there. But I'm also underneath the old pump at the Priory in the corner – and I catch a whiff of wisteria. I inhale it deeply. It clasps the bricks of the tower. Beautiful bursts of mauve and rich scent even in winter. Flowers twice. Late summer too, I think. What am I doing there at the bottom of the well? I don't know. But I'm feeling the emptiness and exploring a shape to it. Still no sense of it really – I only know it feels like nothing. No inclination. No impulse. No suggestion. Really, nothing there. No flourishes, no edge down which to shoot, no shape or dimension, no holder or ballast. No laughter or play. No content to distract or story to transport. Only the memory of wisteria, living on as a fragment of perfume, sludgy old water stagnant with rotting leaves and squelchy bits – a dead end here. No further to go. One more step. One more.

Until nothingness wasn't anything anymore.

At some point, impossible to locate in time, a glow swelled at my feet in the cold darkness of the *baño*. A luminous presence was kneeling down before me. I knew at once what it was: it was me, an aspect of my being, from the future, there to retrieve me, to return me to the only place I truly belonged. "Come," it said. "Breathe. I have come back for you. You have forgotten we have another life, from another time and place to return to. This is not what we are choosing."

There was more purging but of no consequence. After six months of wandering blindly, enchanted by the beauty and menace of the jungle, I had been spat out. I was back. Candles were lit, the hut returning to a place of solid walls and beams, sheltering thatch; the faces of everyone telling their own story of what the medicine had inspired and exacted from them. Chatter, stretching, yawns and whispers, laughter; some faces were pinched or drawn, others wide awake, attuned to bliss, community, possibility.

The head shaman El Maestro walked past my seat where I was too dazed and weak to move. "At last, Mags," he said, not disguising a smile. "You arrived with 98% bullshit. Now you know it and that bullshit can clear." My move through darkness had been endorsed.

The door to freedom, I was soon to realise, had been opened ajar. I had seen what darkness was. I knew what it could be, and how the world mirrored back whatever you held within you, including what was ready to be faced. What sounded or looked brutal was no more no less than an echo of the expelling judgments deep within my being. In the language of warriorship, the system I'd tried so hard to uphold, defence was a tool of war – rooted in the same fear as the attack goading it. Where was the peace in that? A turning point had come. I no longer intended to invite any more egocentric phantoms into my life or their armoured front any longer. After all, having faced my own hollowed integrity, why would I need to? The forward motion that had been so developed in me, steeped in aspiration and goals, was beginning to fall apart. It was time to begin living another way.

There was then, at that time and place downstream, an

opening for Grandmother to keep watch, until I was ready to hear her calling. We had yet to meet. I can now see the bigger thread that had always tethered me to her, no matter how lost I had felt myself to be. There was no such thing as a tidily wrapped story and finishing line, after all. Within weeks of that fateful night, I had moved on, the chapter as an aspiring Ayahuascera closed.

Chapter 10

Wild Heart

Several thousands of miles upriver, white-capped peaks encircle a lesser-known sacred site among Peru's world-class lexicon. The ancient temple at Chavin has an intimate ambience, older and less visited than Machu Picchu. The mountains resemble grand curtains parted for sacred drama, cleaved by a valley down which water careers night and day. Their every face overlooks the source of the Amazon, where the rivers Mosna and Huachecza join. Peru's topography, as I was discovering, demonstrates the worlds of consciousness that its ancient people mapped; the Lower World, or unconscious, the Amazon's muddy swamps, and the Upper World or 'super-consciousness', where eagles soar among snow-capped peaks, expansive and visionary. Those 'Apus' are towering witnesses to the start of the Amazon's long journey to the ocean.

It is at Chavin – birthing a culture that flowered at least ten times longer than the Incas – where the distinctions of height and swamp unite. The denser energy of the jungle seeped into its highland spirit, influencing the way life was seen and how it was expressed. The exotica of plants and animals of wild power enriched the higher spaces of the Gods, stars and their cosmology, to inspire an epoch of creativity, as surviving ceramics and totems testify. Even in such altitude, I could feel the presence of the trees I had worked with, the effects of the strict *dietas*. It was easier now to feel the benefits from the many abstentions we had to make for the spirits held within the barks to take life. They followed me everywhere. The jungle was a living force within me.

At Chavin, the 'Apu' lorded over a perfect alpine theatre that hosted thousands of pilgrims three thousand years ago. They would have come from all over the continent for epic occasions. Unlike most cultures known about, Chavin evolved according to the principles of unity consciousness – decisions reached from the perspective of the whole. For some two thousand years, it was a harmony of peace and democracy, unblighted by war or disease. Without any great drama apparently, it simply disbanded, allowing nature to fill its place and smaller tribal groups.

I was eager to visit the central attraction before it closed for the day, a chamber tucked away at the back of the temple. The main ceremonial square leading to it had a living grandeur. Large steps where the masses would sit were stacked neatly upwards; those of higher quality stone for the dignitaries. Despite an earthquake devastating much of it, a giant doorway for the shamans, the Portada, still stole the scene. It was a harmony of black granite and white limestone, engraved with male and female eagles that looked real enough to take flight at any moment. Everything within the ceremonial practice and iconography honoured the duality of life; the relationship of male and female, earth and sky, life and death. It was a tango playing out in all dynamics, of the staccato and lyrical, a teetering pose or graceful limbo. Beyond the Portada was a building housing tunnels and chambers for meditation; their ventilation shafts and giant granite blocks seamlessly held together would pose an engineering challenge today.

I headed to the galleried chamber where Chavin's stone monolith Lanzón still stood. The tunnel was narrow and musty. Drawing nearer, there was an unsettling anticipation in my stomach, as its form got larger, lit up by an eerie glow of revolving light. I dropped to the dusty stone floor. A glass screen separated the ten-foot distance between us. It had an overpowering vitality, astonishing for something made of stone – and it was little wonder the God had drawn hundreds of thousands of pilgrims to kneel at the engraved claws of its feet. Jaguar and serpent, eagle and condor, plant and cactus fused as one shimmering otherworldly being.

Lanzón was an external emanation of power, mesmerising for the humility it was stirring in me. And I could feel my own heart opening, knowing it was being confronted with a choice: to swallow its authority over my own, or acknowledge the throne within myself I had struggled for so long to claim. Such an altar, like all others, was to inspire devotion of the divine. It was too easy to mistake it for the real thing, as an effigy of fathomless love. Hadn't I given my power away time and again to people who seemed more credible as fonts of wisdom and insight?

It was only a few weeks on since I had left Iquitos. It was a lesson I had to learn at some point, however bitterly – or else different situations and people, boyfriends, employers or gurus would continue to show up until at last I recognised myself as the source of my disempowerment. It was too easy to blame others. It gave away the power to change, reducing me to a loser. Accepting responsibility was not to be begrudged: it was the key to freedom, to choose to live differently. And yet, for all my reflections, I couldn't overturn the Maestro in my heart as a vain, waffly, self-obsessed young twit, as lost as anyone else. It was too soon. It still felt awkward remembering how much I had yearned for his approval during those long months in the Amazon. When it hadn't come, I started to imagine and believe in my own inadequacy. My beliefs amplified everything around me, twisting what I saw, heard or felt to support the thesis – everyone else had an answer. Yes, it was all too tempting, as many religions taught and I had bitterly experienced, to regard the Infinite as something separate and unreachable from myself. Like the shining power and beauty of Lanzón before me.

Empowerment was a perpetual challenge – and did I truly want sovereignty? Was I really willing to give up the drama of my struggle, the spice of conflict, which I loved to think I didn't enjoy, the vitality in charged feeling, to own my full power and take responsibility for my life – all of it? And would such independence, as my own counsel, keep the world at a distance, outlawing life's greatest invitation: intimacy?

I could feel the presence of the ancestors and original maestros of Chavin through the veils of time. Believing in my unworthiness honoured a false god. It was nothing short of 'arrogant' to question my place in the world when everything – every living thing – was perfect at its core. The choice was mine: to give up such falsehoods and start living more authentically. Only then would the door open to the kingdom of bliss that was my right – as much as everyone else's.

I understood Chavin had never stopped being its original inspiration, an expression of the unifying power of love and diversity of creation. Those who built it had infused its every stone with that intent. It embodied an evolving consciousness. No matter how worn and crumbled in places, or emptied in others by earthquake and plunder, the temple lived on, encompassing the heart of the culture that had created it, as well as today's fractured times of volatility and unrest. People and communities were waking up across the globe, crying out for more freedom and autonomy. As Chavin inspired me, so it was inspiring a new story for an emerging humanity – as much outside me as it was part of me.

The next day, I set off early to travel to a magical mountainous sanctuary of ancient lands. The Bosque de las Piedras were slopes of monolithic stones stretching for miles. Exploring them could take days. Each one was unique, as if crafted to convey every state of being. Those stones, according to local lore, were the Earth's first people, sentient as the life to come – the mineral kingdom predating plants by billions of years. As apparently vital as Lanzón, those monoliths were forever rooted, patient and still. At four thousand metres, weather played into a constantly shifting relief. As I wandered, the mist swirled around them to reveal glimpses of their varied natures, before vanishing into time's oblivion once more.

It was in that greyness I was to come face to face with the legend of the Apu – a puma – widely believed to be extinct. Only this mountain cat was very real. I had been roaming for some hours, attuned to the feel of the place, when a sudden tension emanated from within the labyrinth of stones. The atmosphere had shifted – making me stand still and hold my breath. There was an unnatural quiet: the birdsong stopped. Hummingbirds had lined up along the tops of stones, jagged as steeples. The frozen presence of wildlife broadcast something remarkable about to happen. A silhouette of a giant hare emerged through thinning gloom, as still as the boulder it perched upon. It looked too staged to be real; its floppy-eared head tilted in caricature. This was a magical moment, and it was another witness to the imminent physical encounter with the high mountain's most secretive resident.

The cat slinked into view. As quickly as I spotted it, it saw me and we exchanged a long look – enough time to become fully alert to the unlikely chance of our meeting. It was the head of the food chain and artful at concealment. Its sensory powers were undisputed, an ability to track a whiff of prey at least a day's distance away. It was the totem used by shaman in other worlds, so artful a tracker and made of raw strength. In the physical world, in the charged stillness all around me, the puma was also grace itself – the life beholding it knew it too: animal, mineral and human. There – some ten feet apart – her powerful being met mine.

Wild heart, untamed love. Shadowy stalker, stealthy poise. Fierce fighter. Murderous strength. Fearless mistress.

Our eyes locked. A recognition – naked and unending.

Slowly – each moment a frame of muscular tension – the puma looked away and to one side, determining its next move. In a flash, it turned into a blur, scampering back through the maze of pathways, to other territories.

The puma was Chavin's ultimate totem, the most revered embodiment of wild power. The mountain cat was the jungle's sister, but a distinctive creature of the heights; its markings similar, only smaller and more rare still. The feline of swamp and summit was a symbol of the force within all creation. She represented the great feminine being of Mother Nature herself – the yin to the yang of life. It was a gift – a lucky chance – that I had felt her looking into me so fully. Where did her wild heart and untameable grace live on in me?

Was it then or later on – that the skies started opening up in the moody space of the Bosque de las Piedras? As they cleared, a rainbow arced across, vividly bridging one soil to another, its middle smudged by cloud. It reminded me of the arc of each and every life, only its bookends of birth and death assured. The mystery lay in between; hidden, until it had revealed itself whole.

Chapter 11

Friendly Ghosts

After my trip to Chavin to honour the Amazon's source, the very spot where the mighty river began its long journey to the ocean, there was one more destination in my sights in Peru. I would then cross into Bolivia and Lake Titicaca for the last leg of my travels, to visit a sacred site eclipsing Machu Picchu in importance – a temple at the zenith of Incan spiritual culture, on the Island of the Sun. As the most venerated force in creation, the Incas believed they descended from the sun's brilliant light, to which they would return. The temples on that island were their ultimate pilgrim destination. Going there, as I imagined it, would be my own pilgrimage to crown everything experienced in the last year before returning home. First I wanted to prepare by fasting for seven days, ingesting water only. Less than half a day's travel from the Bolivian border, Sillustani in Peru's south-eastern tip seemed the perfect place to go. Isolated but accessible, it was a peninsula, nestled between small communities. It was also an ancient burial site.

From a distance the pepper pot structures known as 'chulpas' towered over the skyline, some taller and grander than others, depending on the seniority of those buried there. There were dozens of them, every large stone seamlessly layered. It was first recognised by the warrior tribe, the Colla, and then the Incas for its spiritual power. Surrounded by water, it was hard to imagine a more tranquil setting to honour the dead. Dragonflies and butterflies accompanied me as I wandered among the *chulpas* looking for a spot to pitch my tent. Silently, I asked the spirit of the place for three signs to show beyond doubt I was welcome at Sillustani to hold my fast.

As I clambered down one of the hillsides, at the back of the site, hundreds of exotic green birds rose into the sky, shocked out of their grassy resting place. They flew away en masse, a fluttering emerald green sheet. They were 'pilco', birds venerated by the Incas. I also knew the last of the three gateways on the Island of the Sun was built to honour the *pilco*. Many pilgrims used to be turned back at that final screening of their worthiness to continue on to the main temple. They were beautiful to behold, resembling for a moment an unbroken swathe of airborne grass. I stood enthralled until the last shining green bird had disappeared. Barely drawing breath, I faced a new surprise: two eagles flying overhead, from left to right, then circling together high above. Birds of prey were synonymous with visionary power. They were spiritual messengers too for the ancients. Neither spectacle could be dismissed as chance – and together, they mirrored back to me the synchronous power of intention. The spirit of the place and its unseen intelligence could not be ignored. No sooner had the soaring eagles left, a frantic squawking turned my attention directly above, as four birds glided towards each other from the four directions. They seemed to hover in a square before coming together, gently brushing wing against wing as if in an orchestrated dance. At the moment of touch, they released three feathers. I counted again to make sure – it was hard to accept the realness of such seamless wonders. As the birds flew away, the feathers drifted to the ground in small arcs – cradled by the air's resistance. Believe in magic, I mused, and magic happens. The extraordinary and ordinary were life's dance-fellows, so easily blurred together. One could elevate and enliven, the other deflate or dull – it was a matter of perception. To play my part, I had to remember to keep open to mystery. The ancestors, I felt certain, were encouraging me to stay. What was more, by chance, my six nights would coincide with a full moon, allowing the water to glisten at night with an eerie brilliance.

I scanned the terraced slope. There was a choice of flat areas sheltered by boulders, good shade from the sun. As I pitched my tent that first day, the hunched profile of an elderly man waved down at me. I scrambled up to him, where he greeted me warmly and asked if he could help in any way. When I explained I was there to fast for a week, he nodded knowingly, and offered to visit me once a day with a flask of hot water. He was one of the guardians of the ancient site. His job was to guide visitors and share the small knowledge about the more important people buried there, according to rank and custom.

Those seven days were a meander through profound peace. Every day I sat entranced by a flat-topped island directly opposite. Strikingly straight, it could have been sheared by a razor. At night, there were many storms. The moon's orb would radiate a silver glow from behind thick clouds, always cleared by morning. Everyday the water lapped gently against the shore, perfectly fresh for my early morning bathe. Some days I'd barely move, others I would burn off huge energy roaming among the *chulpas*, exploring their secret nooks. There was nothing spooky about them. The site honoured the dead with a consideration that could still be felt. My own mind stilled in the uniquely tranquil ambience. There was nothing I wanted or missed, with one exception. During the full moon, succulent chunks of pizza and cheesecake haunted me, and I punished myself with salivating fantasies of menus in tourist restaurants I would soon visit. Once I saw how hunger was a projection of mind, the effect was dramatic. My thoughts lost their power and my empty stomach no longer bothered me.

The only other ripple to upset my equilibrium was to be woken up on three consecutive nights by something wriggling beneath me. I felt it move stealthily along my body, with only the thin canvas layer separating us. On one occasion, there were three such lumps – beneath my shoulder, leg and cheek. I felt unconcerned, imagining a few sweet mice comforted by warmth. The next day the mystery was solved, not without drama.

Wandering up the slope, taking all the time my fasting body wanted, I glanced down at the rock where my sandaled foot was about to land, and screamed at what I saw. My toes were within a few inches of a large furry tarantula. It was a shock to behold its fleshy body and legs, still and poised. Tarantulas lived in the jungle, but at altitude? In the exotic setting of the Amazon, at a guarded distance, they looked handsome in their rightful place. Not there, in the dry mountain region of peace-filled Sillustani. A sudden thought made me scream again, as the full horror dawned. My nocturnal visitors weren't small hamster-like rodents after all – but tarantulas.

The discovery was surprising: it had taken me at least an hour tracking the perfect camping site that felt just right. Aside from physical details, the land could feel very particular from one spot to the next. In the end my tent was pitched on ground feeling unmistakably different from that a few metres away. When laying out the tent, I had spotted three little holes and assumed they housed the tiniest vole. One was between my inner and outer tent. Gazing at the tarantula sprawled on the rock, not wanting to let it out of my sight, I pictured my bare feet stomping over that very hole time and again. Arachnophobic, I had gravitated to the one spot on the mountain that, it was to turn out, had three tarantula nests within tent-sized distance. Later, as I searched for a new tarantula-free zone to relocate, no matter how hard I looked, there were no other holes to be found. For all the repulsion arachnids inspired in me, I had been drawn to the one place where they amassed. Remarkably, nowhere else felt as 'right' as that first site. Attraction and repulsion could feel so similar. They were strange bedfellows, holding the same magnetic energy. One was a shadowy twin, tailing wherever the other shone, resistance making its magnetism all the stronger. Only later could I know this of Grandmother – that her life-death call could never be suppressed indefinitely. She was lurking in the shadows, waiting, for all my denial of our inevitable encounter. At some point, fear had to be faced. Life demanded growth, to challenge the comfort zone keeping me safe and small. How much arachnids teach me in their bold unpredictable scuttle. Their eight legs weave a powerful dance that triggers a primal horror in me, which no amount of appropriate thinking can overwrite. Only there, at Sillustani, as I saw them then, long before my first encounter with Grandmother, I didn't realise how much they held the story of my fear of death itself. They were a physical inconvenience for their ugliness, as well as a curious contradiction, given how much I seemed to be drawn to their energetic signature. I could acknowledge this at a contented distance. Handling them was another matter.

I was never on my own for long at Sillustani. Not only a daily visit from the old man with a flask of hot water – but one night I woke up to the sound of shredding paper outside my tent. My stomach plunged – I was a good half hour's walk from the nearest house. I lay still trying to imagine what it could be. Summoning the courage, I opened the outer tent to investigate. An emaciated stray dog looked up at me, a little bemused, and began to pant from the hard work of shredding newspaper scavenged from my rucksack. Clothes lay scattered about, the dog having managed to drag the pack outside the flysheet. He'd traced the scent of some offerings stuffed inside – stale chocolate, biscuits and coca leaves. Somehow he had found me, drawn to another hungry and solitary being. From then on, we were inseparable; every night he'd settle down to sleep next to me, never leaving my side until I finished the fast – two perfectly matched companions connected by the twists of circumstance.

Even without my canine ally, I felt the presence of friendly spirits among the *chulpas*. I had limited direct experience of death, too young to have really mourned my grandparents. Two friends had died as teenagers. With my shamanic work, I often supported people with issues around dying, or bereavement. Most of what I had learnt was inspired by ancient cultures. Death was celebrated as the birth of new life, as an integral part of its passage. Grieving was all part of that ritual. Elaborate prepara- tions were made for a soul's onward journey. I'd studied pyramids and tombs, from Mexico to Peru, Greece, India, Egypt and Tibet. Death was held as the ultimate gateway illuminating universal mysteries inaccessible in life. Ayahuasca, the 'Vine of the Soul', as I had experienced, opened up those very same psychic dimensions.

At Sillustani, roaming among friendly ghosts, the contrast with my own encounters with death could not have been more dramatic. There was such finality beholding coffins at the front of a crematorium or church – never feeling moved by the few funerals I had attended. Death felt distant, clinical even – having taken place behind hospital doors, or relayed over a phone. As a journalist, reporting death or murder was routine. It was statis- tical or swiftly eclipsed by other events. I remembered the half day spent at a mortuary, researching the role of a coroner's officer. The pathology unit, white tiled throughout, had rows of trolleys with corpses covered in starched sheets. They were a lot to get through – each one unloaded in turn on to shiny metal surfaces for examination. The pathologist was efficient, pulling a sheet back in one quick stroke and glancing at her clipboard, an array of tools at hand.

There was nothing generous about death's finishing touches; mountainous stomachs bloated with gases, streaks of purplish skin in mottled white flesh, the same plastic quality of a mannequin. No incense, flowers, chanting or dignity. The details of dying were so glaringly inevitable and so unimaginable at the same time – the wedding rings still worn, the sunken chins, jaws collapsed with the dentures out, the limp hair – a bland spectacle of the everyday. Those were details most would never think about, struggling to preserve a memory of how loved ones were in life. That was the most surprising part to my day among the corpses: the banality of dying, at its most physical. All mystique was wiped away with every sanitising stroke of the mortuary technician's mop, over the crusty brown blood and intestinal debris. It was fascinatingly routine. I couldn't stare hard enough.

The coroner's officer, who had shared several macabre assumptions, such as "this one liked a few burgers," then rolled in a trolley – a road victim. Nineteen years old. It was only when I thought of his parents answering the telephone that fateful day, the news broken to them, that I remembered how death could mean something else entirely. It was no longer a process, clinical or biological. It was an event, labelled tragic. It was something unfair. It was a lament over time's passing, a lonely curse at being left behind. It was perhaps a chance to lace up the deceased's life story – no longer someone difficult, selfish, or whatever. Death was whatever it was made to mean. There was the pathologist, showing no signs of fatigue, her plastic gloved hands stuffing back internal body parts into the corpse, that had been a father, a wife, a sister, a son, then reaching out for the medical sewing kit to stitch up an afternoon's work.

It wasn't cynical. Heartlessness did not come into it. There was a cultural instinct in the West towards preserving life at all cost, not the sacredness of its passing. The death rites I had learnt practised by the Qu'ero Indians in the Andes transcended physical realities but didn't try to tidy them away either. The moment of physical death was for many ancient cultures a transition – an ultimate rite of passage which could deepen a soul's journey through the ongoing dimensions of eternal life. The more sacred the manner of an individual's passing, the more death could be embraced as an opening of consciousness and opportunity for transformation. That took preparation. The energetic body could be cleared and prayed over by a shaman as the physical body shut down. The afterlife was mapped into recognisable stages of an ongoing journey. Death for the Qu'ero was as much a cause for celebration as mourning, as the beginning as well as ending it was seen to be.

At Sillustani, I was also preparing for what lay ahead, a journey into the very heart of Incan cosmology and how it lived on. What ghosts from my history stalked me that I had yet to lay to rest – like the tarantula whose home I'd chosen unconsciously to sleep on? I had encountered the mountain puma – its spirit sacred to the Inca and more ancient cultures as a powerful guide to track what had to die and be honoured for new life to emerge. Regret still stalked me sometimes, a shadow from the months spent in the jungle, for broken dreams and gaps left by their loss. What other old ghosts might rise to haunt me in the last phases of my adventure? What secrets did Lake Titicaca guard – its waters merging with the mythical lore of the Gods?

Water was the elemental temple of emotions, housed by the West, in the Incan tradition. A shadowy realm of sunsets, the West initiated a pilgrim into the mysteries of death – not only as a gateway to the afterlife, but to welcome the living ghosts, waiting to be honoured. For there was little distinction between life and death back then – temples as much for the business of living as well as dying, for celebration and solemnity, the inexorable partners along the wheel of time. By the end of my fast at Sillustani, I felt ready to deepen my own initiation into the watery worlds of the West – for all the calm and turbulence they were bound to promise.

Chapter 12

Children of the Sun

It had been a cold evening on the Island of the Sun. Lake Titicaca, usually a shimmering azure mirror, was creased with white-capped waves. From my guesthouse I watched the fishing boats rocking in the shallows. The wind had struck up during the boat ride there, the last that day from Copacabana, tucked within the Bolivian border. It was quickly evident the island's name was perfect for one so bleached and bald. The winding paths, the island's only thoroughfares, were walled with large slabs of stone and overrun with geckos. As dusk fell, the hum of generators started up and dots of light joined one home to the next. Without moonlight, the narrow and uneven pathways between had disappeared in the dark. Horseback, boat or foot the only ways to explore, this rustic isolation was perfect to wind up the vibrant and challenging year, my last stop in Latin America before home.

The wind rising, it was too cheerless to stay out watching the horizon blacken, and I turned in early. A hanging bulb cast a cold glare about my room, not inviting me to keep awake. Despite the thin mattress on wooden planks, I managed to fall asleep listening to a shutter squeak in the rising wind.

I woke with a start – stomach tight, breathing shallow. The gale was clattering against the tin roof, waves pounding on the beach. My sheets were dry. The wall I reached for was solid. I was really there in the room – this was real – but the dream had been more real still.

A monstrous black wave had risen out of flat water. It grew until its full height, some seventy, eighty feet high. Its fall was inevitable and with it the destruction of everything around. Panic spread as the wave hovered about to bear down; hundreds of women screaming and running as I watched on hopelessly. They were apparitions of other times and places in my life – acquaintances, close friends, teachers, employers, strangers and sisters. The wave was to wipe them out and the scraps of memory where they lived in me. I rushed to an old red telephone kiosk, to reassure my parents I was still alive. As I dialled their number, the wave finally crashed on to the shore with murderous power. My last thought was to realise I was no longer the child I had been.

I lay haunted by the dream, listening to the shrieking wind. There had been a message: something about waking up, no longer the child I had been. The wave had obliterated any trace of my life, as I had tried to ring my parents to let them know I was safe. It seemed to say I was as much a daughter of the paternal authority embedded in the lore of the Island of the Sun, as I was of two people, as their own flesh and blood. I remembered the medicine of the puma, a powerful shamanic ally in this part of the world. Puma was used to help let go – using her claws to tear away at old, tired stories, and their patterns holding one back. Since my encounter with the mountain cat at Bosque de las Piedras, I was noticing how the past had less of a grip; memories of my challenging time in the Amazon already less uncomfortable than they had been.

It wasn't even midnight. Barely two hours had passed since I had gone to bed. It felt like my psyche had been churned by the tsunami for hours. My bladder was surprisingly full, given how recently I'd turned in. Huddled in a blanket, I faced the inconvenient walk to a toilet.

As I stomped back towards my door, I was startled to see a man sitting cross-legged outside the room next to mine, gazing intently at the storm-whipped lake. He didn't flinch at all from under his traditional wool hat – oddly incurious at the sound of another awake, given how empty the guesthouse seemed. The owner's effusive welcome had made me wonder if anyone had dropped by in months.

Later I woke again and, needing the toilet, ventured out once more. The stars were just as bright and wind as strong. The man hadn't moved, remaining in the same bolt upright posture. Perhaps he was a pilgrim, I decided, showing spirited dedication to his purpose in such a chill. Diving into the heap of blankets again, as I warmed up, the prospect of the day ahead exploring the island's famous ruined temple had lost all appeal.

The alarm pierced me out of sleep. It was eerily quiet, the storm over. Peering out of the curtain, charcoal-grey clouds swirled over a rising sun like a scorpion's tail. My landlady scrambled some eggs, and gave me directions for a shortcut to the ruins. Over a hill and arid fields beyond. Keep going, she pointed vaguely, until you find the original Inca trail, an hour that way, maybe longer.

After gathering my things, I shut my door behind me, as some cheerful whistling started up next door. It represented everything I couldn't summon within me. The same man who'd been up all night breezed past and greeted me with a warm: "Buenos dias," resuming his whistle to the bathroom, a towel swinging over his shoulder. His contentment and easy manner made me aware of how heavy-limbed and dull I felt, setting off in the pathless direction to the ruins.

Nothing seemed beautiful that early morning; clumps of eucalyptus too common to be remarkable. The butterflies and birdsong only compounded my low spirits. Clambering over large boulders, I caught frustrating glimpses of arable green in the dreariness – the Inca path remaining illusive.

A drone of chatter rose from a small field of maize. Some youths were toiling on their haunches, hunched into the soil. I asked the way to the pilgrim's path. They glanced up and burst out laughing before resuming their work as if nothing had happened. I tried again. The question was every bit as funny as before. As I lingered, clearly reluctant to move on without an answer, one of them shook his head and pointed back down the hill towards the coast. How was this possible, I muttered, given my landlady had been very clear of the direction to take? Knowing I was the object of their ridicule, their fresh laughter loud and shrill, my composure cracked.

Everything was conspiring to make me regret ever having set foot on the Island of the Sun. I could picture my sullen face to their mocking eyes. It was absurd to stray from one of the most well known paths on the South American continent, on a tiny island. My strangled voice barked out my most disparaging Spanish, which to exacerbate my annoyance amounted to "rude and unkind". Their behaviour, I added as a final shot, was not "acceptable". More hilarity, doubling-over and hands banging the earth; more tension unleashed in a childlike rant of Spanish and English. Aware of my mad spectacle as a furious *gringa*, I stormed off back down the hill. There was clarity at last: the trip was over.

A whistle stopped me in my tracks. I recognised the teenage son of the guesthouse owner waving at me from beneath a tree. He hurried over with a scrawny boy, introduced as his cousin. I motioned to the youths already bent over their work; the confrontation with a crazed woman apparently forgotten.

"They were lying to you," he said gently. "You just need to keep going. See over there?" He gestured to another slope veering north. "The path is only another five, ten minutes from that point. Follow me."

Immediately my spirits rose. The young cousin tore ahead. The older kept turning round to reassure me we were on course. The pilgrim trail flashed ahead, like a golden ribbon slicing through rubbly contours. I insisted on tipping him, to his awkward surprise. He had simply been showing me the way, he pointed out, like anyone would.

The sun was already strong. The rich blue water encircling me was calm and clear, as if I'd imagined the long wild night. At this point, the Incan pilgrims had been nearing their most sacred temple; the view changed little in the five hundred years since – distant snow-capped peaks and low-lying islands, like smaller siblings. The Island of the Sun crowned their civilisation, for little more than its one hundred year long empire. In that short time, they were industrious, erecting temples and settlements – such as on this land, the home of their fabled Sun God Inti. Scanning south-east, I could make out the Island of the Moon, where Mama Quilla lived, the consort of Inti. Legend had it they were man's original parents. From Titicaca sprung their child, Time, for life to unfold. The sun was revered for being the only element in creation without a shadow; as 'children of the sun', the Incas saw their essence as the same – brilliant light. At the end of their life on Earth, they would return to that very disc of golden fire, beating down on me with unforgiving glare.

I was reaching the last of three gateways before the main complex. Only the purest pilgrims, those vetted by High Priests, were admitted to the principal temple beyond this point, where ceremonies were held for the most enlightened. Given my shaky composure since arriving, I wouldn't have made it far beyond the landing point in the island's south. Since arriving, I had struggled to feel at home on the famed island. The storm, the dream, the youths and even the sun too had seemed not only unfriendly but hostile.

At the temple entrance, the sun shone with more force, the air searing-dry, and it was not yet nine. Stone stairs descended to the ceremonial site, which would usually be swamped with boatloads of visitors. It was deserted, my visit coinciding with a day of local elections all over Bolivia. My priority was to find 'Titi Khar'ka', the rock of the puma. Facing due west, the walled altar was one of the site's highlights.

An old man approached me with a bundle of tourist tickets. I didn't have any change to buy one, and headed to a hut with a generous choice of provisions to break a note: bottles of cola and water, tubes of Pringles crisps and a variety of Western chocolate.

It was strange to encounter such choice in a dusty shack at least an hour's walk from the nearest village. My eyes settled on a family-sized bar of Toblerone, a perfect indulgence after my travelling austerities. Before returning to the ticket vendor, I ripped open the large gold bar. Without a thought, I polished off three large nougat triangles within seconds.

The famous altar was a giant rock resembling the gaping mouth of a large wild cat. Jaguar and its puma sister were believed to be guides through the shadowy territories in life and death. Their medicine for the shamanic culture of the Incas, as I had been taught, was to track ensnaring dramas and their emotional fallout. The seesaw between power and impotence, as human history testified, was seductive territory, requiring the support of the fiercest archetype to navigate through it. Close to where I sat was a stone table the Incas used for human sacrifice, a ritual reserved only for the most auspicious events or ceremonies. The Incan empire grew decisively in a matter of decades, such was the strength of its military government. It was a familiar story: greed and power were endemic within the human race. When had there not been war, annihilation and megalomania throughout schoolroom history? Capitalism was another vehicle for those same seeds, flowering as inequality, starvation and greed. I felt a rising flush of anger. Nothing had evolved during the era of Homo sapiens – and I was just as guilty of self-seeking gratification. I reached for the Toblerone and devoured the last of it.

It was very hot. The sun was boring down from its highest point. I stood up, restless, overwhelmed with irritation for the hallowed site. This might have been a magnet for hundreds of thousands of seekers – but not for me! I headed due east, over a desert of rocks and cacti. At the easternmost point, I scrambled along a cliff, enjoying the freedom of climbing up and down. High above the crystalline water, my legs dangled free over the edge. For the first time that day, a peace settled over me – sitting mesmerised by the lake's vivid blue calm, swelling over rocks resembling the serrated scales of a primeval beast.

How many civilisations had this lake witnessed rise and fall? The Earth was a sad reflection of her relentless plunder. Were the hurricanes her rage, earthquakes her anger, and tsunamis her tears, neglected by those she sheltered and fed? We were tenants of the Earth, not her masters. But remembering this debt began with me. Judging or moaning, railing or lecturing was too easy: it abdicated my responsibility. I had come to the Island of the Sun as the last sacred place on a journey through the millennia of ancient Peru. Over the months in the Amazon I had indulged outrage and regret. Whenever I judged the world 'out there', I was overlooking the world within me. The Earth could be no more separate from me than I was to it. To show the environment disrespect was bound to manifest as a similar disregard for my own balance and dignity. Consuming not only too much but the wrong things ravaged my own body as well as the planet's. I walked on.

Later, nearing the island's outermost point, the presence of the ancestors radiated like a force field. For the first time since stepping on the island, I felt my arrival fully, connected at last to its spirit. I was no longer an aspiring pilgrim with a plan – but a visitor open to everything the island inspired – including my anger, impatience and ingratitude. Whispering into cocoa leaves as offerings, as many shamans had done holding space for me, I apologised for the arrogance and lack of respect I'd shown that day. I pictured myself wolfing down the Toblerone, without any inclination to offer it up first, or feel amazement for its unlikely manifestation. I thanked the ancestors for enabling me to be heard, for allowing me to reach them and see them.

In the stillness, I heard their voices as clearly as my own. "We welcome you, our daughter, because you ate the Toblerone. We thank you for the realness of your endeavour."

What peace in the sweetness of acceptance! Being real, for all my obvious lack of polish, had forged a resonance with the environment and its hidden dimension. The connection felt true to me – not rooted in the flattery of my ego's deluded thinking. At that very moment, an enchanting melody of a flute was carried along on a breeze. It was like an invitation, beckoning me to complete my own undertaking to immerse in the site. Feeling light, bowing to my invisible witnesses, I raced towards the stone labyrinth. I could picture the feathered headdresses and gold ceremonial gear of those once assembled there. Drawn to lie on one of the stone tables, I experienced the gentle touch of those original healers. The afternoon slipped away. As I roamed about, different tourists approached me, asking to explain the layout and function of the site. Feeling so much at home, I pointed out the difference between my own impressions and what I'd read. The sun began to set and the rock of the puma glowed in the crimson-orange light.

It was dark when I stepped through the gate to the guest-house. The landlady rushed out to greet me. She'd been worried – away the whole day! I thanked her for the directions, and yes, the ruins were as beautiful as she'd said. Her son emerged from the kitchen, surprised to see me back so late. The trout I'd ordered at breakfast was almost ready and would be served in ten minutes. He ushered me to my seat that had been laid opposite another, the other guest.

The door swung open, and the man who'd been out all night strode in. Introducing himself as Carles, he extended a hand to shake mine. I couldn't quite believe it was the same man I'd seen. In perfect English he promptly pointed out he was "Catalan, not Spanish – please!" He'd lived in Edinburgh for a couple of years studying film, after finding himself too sentimental to be cut out for a veterinary career. Animals dying in his care had broken his heart every time. As we feasted, I heard about his flourishing writing career: two anthologies of poetry published, and a volume of short stories he was on the island to finish. Apparently

I'd been the first visitor at the guesthouse since his arrival a month before. Carles was curious about the ruins, and admitted he hadn't got round to spending time at them yet.

"So, you're not a pilgrim, then?" I asked.

"Oh no. I'm here for the peace, to finish that book of stories I started a decade ago. I practise yoga and meditate sometimes – but don't really have any deep spiritual connection."

I thought of him, facing the storm and wild water, in the posture of serious contemplation. "But you have affinity," I pointed out. "I mean, you must have been sitting up outside your door for hours last night from what I saw. Were you seeking inspiration for your writing?" I told him about my interrupted night and the two wind-battered visits to the bathroom. My companion stared at me, astonished. He denied it was him. I persisted, describing his hat – the patterns, its flaps, the poncho I'd seen.

"That is my hat, and yes, my poncho – but it wasn't me," Carles retorted. "I hate the dark – it frightens me." He was adamant he would have to be paid to sit up through a storm. It had in fact driven him to the warm comfort of his bed. And, in case I wondered, he had never sleepwalked either. Perhaps a weird stranger had sat outside his door for some reason – should we not be worried?

In a flash, this oddest twist began to make sense. Since setting off for the Island of the Sun, I'd brushed against the hidden mysteries of the sacred island, and the waters surrounding it. My dream had seemed as real as anything I had experienced that day – it felt like a brutal clearance of attachments and identities I'd harboured for as long as I could remember. Time and place didn't follow everyday rules. Who was to say the Carles I had seen wasn't an imprint from the future – a flash of events still to unfold upstream in the chronology of time's river? There was no neat linearity to explain events. My imminent death in the tsunami dream had brought me back to a time existing before the multiple identities that were to define my life. What was more, it allowed me to see this man's shadow – the part of himself he was too afraid to own; the one that loved to roam freely and fearlessly, at one with the unruliness of nature. As Carles denied it within himself, so it lived on, stalking him. I had seen it, witnessing it as clearly as its twin eating opposite me. "No, it was you," I answered, no longer eager to convince him. "There is no doubt about it. You see, that was your shadow. Don't worry," I said, tucking into more trout, "we all have one of those."

Chapter 13

Rendezvous with Grandmother

Sometimes I see myself as a caged bird longing to sing. The instinct for flight, the expansion promised, holds the secret of my heart's yearning to express. What is its song? As I struggle to find its voice, I can become lost in the song of different birds. No matter how much they touch vast vistas in me, the discovery of my own is the most inspiring. It is the key to opening the door pinning my wings, to freedom the other side.

The story of 'my song' begins with my earliest memory: witnessing life around me, as I woke up from a sleep. I remember the very moment I became aware of a separate world. A blast of sensory data. No language for any of the things I noticed or the feelings excited in me. The story has since fleshed out: it was an afternoon, and I was in a pram beneath a magnolia tree. The leaves were waxy green – as I have verified from seeing them many times since, bursting into flower twice a year. They belong to the sturdy trunk that to this day climbs up the 'Priory's' front wall. This awakening happened when I was a baby, between eighteen and twenty-two months old. Developmental science has located this period during which an ego is born – a separation from everything else, in which a 'me' springs and 'you' or 'it' also appear.

My first memory was the Big Bang moment birthing 'me'. Until then, despite what others have claimed, I wasn't there. Whatever was there didn't know of 'here' – despite official accounts recording the contrary. A date, place and name identified the 'it' and registered its birth – recording its unique life in time, which in fact began many months later in its own true experience of waking up to this world. It's been my word over anyone else's ever since. Somewhere in all this remembering, I got lost in the story of others – mistrusting the barometer of my own sensory mechanism and its intelligence, my bodily experience. As I grew up, my instinct and trust in it was overshadowed by reason – two very different narrators of life's unfolding.

Many years later, an established adult, apparently rational and responsible, another 'Big Bang' moment woke me up to a whole new universe. This time, deep in the Amazon, I began to emerge from another sleep – the waking dream of ordinary reality. It had been just as befuddling as a baby's bewitchment by the life it discovers for the first time. The jungle was to inspire another perspective on how everything outside and inside 'me' were not in any way separate – but woven together, a seamless continuum. That sense of oneness was harder to relate to the choppier human dynamics I encountered there. My experience had often told me something else no matter how loving the company around me. Still, the Amazon's compelling magic had swept away my innocent acceptance of what the world seemed to be. My whole outlook began to teeter: all the projections, beliefs and assumptions upon which my life had drawn meaning. I had placed my total faith in a world and its customs so very different from the one my infantile senses had first beheld – uncorrupted then by any influence. The world is at once a collective one, pummelled and pinched into a commonly witnessed landscape, more credible and real than the fairy tale one taking life beneath it.

Who am I without the beliefs that make one story more real than all the others – as free as light itself? In this one, Grandmother's white head of hair was aglow with coppery strands glinting in the sun. The bun came undone and her curls fell to the ground, dispersing from her feet as writhing snakes. Her eyes glared green, cold and reptilian. It was an effort adapting to Grandmother's shifting shape. Our communication was unstable and I wanted her to settle down a bit. My wish was granted. Grandmother, as she'd been that first meeting among the apple trees, was back, this time in a memorable outfit – a purple turtleneck jumper, kilt and sturdy lace-up shoes. "Shall we go for a walk?" she suggested, sounding unmistakably Scottish.

"I'd like that," I replied.

"Just one last tweak, if you'll allow me," she teased, narrowing one eye in a quasi-wink. Her hair turned lurid pink before my eyes, as if an invisible paint pot had been tipped over it. "I do like to make an effort for an outing," she confided excitedly, her accent decisively Glaswegian.

Together we strolled along a desert of sandy flats, harbouring fossils as old as time. The sea shone silver in the distance as the sun glared from its noon zenith. I wondered why I was not overheating, given the circumstances. From nowhere, Grandmother offered me an ice cream cone with a yellowy swirl of cream, studded with black vanilla flecks. "Sugar, a legally-sanctioned drug, is the biggest threat to your world and its progress through time," she declared, still assuming the voice of a Scottish elder. "But with me now, no harm can come."

We wandered along silently, the ice cream tasting of caramelised buttercups, with a hint of peppery spice, the most exquisite, exciting flavour ever to melt in my mouth. "You're wondering if I exist as an independent being, or…"

"… if I've made you up!" I finish.

"You have to get beyond this 'what is real' malarkey! All life is a story. There is no thing that is not made up."

Stories. I tried to imagine a life without them. A bald commentary of fact, one after the other: A Cup Is. No nuance from words or deception to appearances. No relationship to personalise, insult or aggrandise the little me. A world without texture, emptied of perception and comparison.

"You passed a test in the Hallway of Mirrors at Mount Bugarach."

"Really?"

"You recognised yourself as the great reflection of the infinite mind. Life in all its parts staring back at you, as 'you' remembering yourself as 'everything'."

"That's not true. There were things down there I can't accept, that will never be me."

"All life is a mirror of your own. The bigger is a reflection of the smaller. Wanting anything to be other than what it is, is a projection of your own will to write a new story. You are the world remembering the world is in you! The idea that life should conform to the narrowest conception of 'ideal' is to swallow the lie there is anything more to be, anywhere better to go, anything more to do. Look..."

Grandmother bent down, her ice cream enjoyed some time ago, and drew a circle in the sand with one large finger. She split it with a line down the middle, and shaded one side, leaving the other clear.

"That's you, dear."

"Two half-circles?"

"One half is the part you know all about, you've accepted. It's allowed to engage with the projected critics known as 'others', 'the world' or 'society'. The other is the banished part – waiting in the Hallway of Mirrors, a library of all the selves to be remembered, welcomed back into the whole you or full circle."

"But that can't include everything? There has to be some discrimination."

"A vacuum is created by judging yourself and others, and all the assumptions and beliefs hacking apart your unlimited nature."

"But what would happen if I welcomed the racist, terrorist and abuser with open arms? How can that be at all useful to civilised society?"

"Until you make a commitment to see yourself in all things, you will continue to live in the self-styled hell you call normal life. Loneliness is confused thinking – believing yourself separate from everything else. Opening the heart makes you one with all nature."

"I'm not ready to make that step."

"That is not true. I couldn't be here unless you had summoned me to tell you what you need to hear."

"I've summoned you?"

"Yes and no. You've called on me to remind you pursuing peace and happiness over the less feel-good emotions will unleash catch-up later on. The rest, bubbling down there, will erupt until it sees the light of day. The lava field is not only beneath Bugarach but in you. The unconscious part of yourself, here – "

Grandmother tapped the shaded half of the circle with her sensible laced shoe. "... This part of you, has been creating your life without you even knowing it. It draws events, circumstances and people into your life – without your knowing consent."

I thought how I could relate that to the habits and tendencies so hard to break. The fits and starts of enthusiasm. Putting authority or someone's talents on a pedestal – projecting power outside myself as exclusive and unobtainable.

"You no longer want to live from that part – the part that sleeps, while thinking you're living from here." Her stockinged foot switched sides. "The patterns you have created – unconsciously – will keep producing the same villains, unfulfilling relationships, the unsustainable enthusiasms, warring thoughts and sabotaging beliefs that leave you asking, time and again...?" Grandmother looked at me sweetly, inviting me to finish.

"What am I doing here – again?"

"Exactly! You yearn to love more deeply... and the connection with all life your heart craves, your song bursting to sing in the world, can only be realised by...?" Grandmother held my gaze, fiercely this time.

"By..." I mimicked, disliking where I thought she might be leading me.

"By descending to rescue the parts of yourself that have been abandoned, judged, spurned, relegated, burned, trashed, spat upon, denied, jilted, divorced, neglected, shamed, ridiculed, tortured, worshipped, adored, envied, trusted, cradled... and exiled. Then, your unique song gets richer, its tones more heavenly!"

"How can that be when it feels so grim down there?"

"That depends on your point of view. The greatest light is there for sure. It is the brightest most humans are terrified to call your own. Instead you fall in love with it, idolise it or vote it into Government, or more commonly, persecute it for shining too brightly."

"And the stuff that isn't desirable?"

"There's such magic to this! By seeing something for what it is, for what it taught you, and feeling the force of life within it once more, makes it transform. It becomes, let us call it, 'spirit gold'. It is the other face of any quality you care to mention. Nothing can exist without its opposite, its shadowy twin. The more your half-circle resembles a full circle, the richer your life becomes."

I remembered Carles sitting up all night, which he had yet to experience for himself. His greatest fear, exposure to the wild spirit of the dark, had taken form – without him knowing it. And I had witnessed this with my own eyes.

"Is this the only way to peace – to face deepest fears and repressions?"

"You have to invite them so they don't spring surprises on you, deary! You must meet them – consciously. The way up is down. And the way forwards, in your case, is also down. Awareness is not enough! If you don't accept all you encounter – not with your mind but your body – and feel through resistance, you will remain a contrived patchwork, a sham. You will love a great deal less than your unlimited heart can love. You will know a fraction of the joy within relationships. You will never delight in the freedom of being the brightest expression of who you choose and experience yourself to be."

"But I've been down there – again and again. What do I have to do differently this time?"

"Face your death."

All the light, all the warmth drained from the space. The sun had become swallowed in grey-crested clouds crumpling the sky as a sea in a storm's approach. "Until you embrace death, you shun life. You live as if you have all the time in the world to indulge your dis-ease. Every moment is precious in all its unedited glory – the frustrations and trials, the hurts and wants! When you know your death is coming, how differently they then seem."

I thought of the Earth spinning on its axis, a globe of mesmerising beauty; how I loved it, roaming among its creased browns, desert fauns, forest greens and pinky flats among the vaster ocean blues. If I knew my time had run out to explore more of the world, how those memories would transform into the richest treasures!

"You have unfinished business in one remaining continent," Grandmother resumed, her tone businesslike. "It is still clouded by unresolved stories that sprung there. You abruptly cut them short. There is, for want of a less loaded word, 'exorcism' to be done. You've already made such a journey before: you revisited the Amazon – to the heart of darkness you had created there. But there is further to go. You have to venture to Tibet this time, and retell the untold story that haunts you as a ghost."

"It does? Which one?"

"The story of your traverse of the Himalayas, to flee from oppressors as an oppressed; risking death over living as if you were dead."

"But I didn't do that. I met plenty who did, but that wasn't actually me."

"Ah, you are mistaken. Their story happened in your world, your universe. It makes it your story."

"That makes no sense," I cried, exasperated. "It happened to someone else, many others in fact – all of them, refugees."

"Some things are forgettable. Others come alive through resonance. You felt and still feel the pain of those people, those refugees you sought out. You identified with their accounts of struggle and deprivation, until their story of endurance became a part of you. You yearned to know the same fearless passion, risking the loss of everything – your own life – never to betray your own heart. That horror and suffering lives in you – that's why they showed up in your universe."

"My universe? They exist in their own right."

"Nothing exists independently! It takes a witness to bring to life the story of its being. You too wander through winters towards freedom. You too are a refugee. You will remain exiled, in failing to meet your truest self, as the full-blooded being you are. Those restless ghosts will stalk you from the shadows, casting ice over your attempts to love."

"And how do I avoid being chased like this – lay them to rest once and for all?"

"You don't avoid their shadows – because you can't. They are as attracted to you as you are repelled by them. Transform them into the richest medicine. Immerse in the fate of the Tibetans who so moved you. Feel every moment of their unending torment by telling their story as if it is your story. Let the spiral take you deeper into its unending revolution. Invite life to express through you all the horror and hell of exile – as you choose to give up the pretence there is any other way!"

The doorways that had appeared at the end of my time in the spiral at Mount Bugarach vividly flashed back. Each one, I had sensed then, was a threshold I had to cross, to transform the story of exile seeded within them. The same signs glowed above each one. Priory. Climbing. Romance. Amazon. Tibet.

The Priory, I could see, was as vital as any living being. Looking over its familiar features, the tower and chimneys, windows and magnolia tree, I felt nothing but happy nostalgia and gratitude for a lifetime's shelter. There was no longer the frisson of attachment, the binding from childhood stunting my growth, which the spiral had shown me at Bugarach. As soon as I acknowledged such sweet peace, the vision disappeared.

Next, 'Climbing' – as I regarded the doorway, the walls of rock or ice in the mountain panorama didn't inspire fear. I could look at them without feeling vertigo or the angst of having to climb them. My relationship to mountains wasn't just about the physical sport. They represented my drive, the struggle of attainment. I could still track a hint of frustration and uncertainty over my desire to find a life purpose. Then again, hadn't I been waking up to being more than the sum of my physical achievements? Possibilities had opened up in Bugarach and the Amazon that could never be measured, unlike a job promotion or pat on the back. Freedom was unquantifiable. It was a state of being.

The doorway framed by 'Romance' I now knew promised a thorny escape from the only sustaining love affair to be had: with myself. Self-reliance required the very trust I had longed to feel in others. It was much lonelier to be in a struggling relationship with another than a committed one with myself. The weight of expectations for a saviour's rescue had crashed in the Amazon; as well as the cold intent to be someone bigger, brighter, and more gifted than I felt myself to be. Both those vibrant thresholds through which I had struggled to escape from my restless heart again disappeared.

One doorway remained: Tibet; the old monk in the shelter, serene and at peace, looking out at the Himalayan skyline. Something stirred in me. What still moved me remembering his story, and those like him, who had abandoned the life they loved and all those in it, so their home would remain an unblemished memory? There was a regret I could feel about such an exile – uprooting from somewhere never to be seen again that would forever hold me, no matter how vast the mountains in between.

"When you die, you will be alone," Grandmother cut in, breezy and matter-of-fact. "Death is the ultimate gateway. No hand can accompany you through it, no matter how tightly it squeezes yours. It is the rarest chance, the greatest gift, to surrender the life that you have lived – to the unknown. Death compels you to forsake everything that has ever handrailed you up the mountains of your own making. Are you willing to die?"

"I know I have to face the ghost of Tibet," I answered.

"First, you will seek the protection of the Elementals – those guardians of the fierce heart. With their help, you must destroy the very contract that has bound you to the constraints of an ordinary life – one flattened and dulled by fear and reason. This contract has to be obliterated – with it, the phantasmagoric self in whom you have such blind faith! Only then will you stand a chance of facing your exile – your ghost in Tibet."

The shadow of a giant bird flew over us. The setting had turned into a colourless wasteland, hopeless and barren; the spirit of death's wake could be felt as a chilling physical presence. "Are you ready to die?" Grandmother persisted, her form as an eccentric old crone fading. She was becoming the wind, a compressed whirling force. Her features shrivelled into angular, desiccated forms, her nose a hooked beak, and tongue slithering in and out of a scaly hole, her voice rasping and shrill. "Face the fear of your own death. It is there, it is, no matter how well hidden it's been!"

My stomach crashed. No more me? The wind rose as the claws of a vulture scraped against my chest. The breeze lifted me off my feet as the landscape around us, the sand and ocean, broke apart, spirited up in the same rising force. All the time I could hear her as a voice within me:

You are playing out exile… among the extremes of your unbridled being. You are yearning for home – and are slowly waking up, remembering where to find it!

Chapter 14

Bewitchment of History

I woke up in a thick wood at the dead of night, lit by the creamy phosphorescence of unending stars. Tilting my gaze, the sky looked alive with movement, crystals of liquid light. A soft high voice unfurled like coiling smoke from far away. Its melody was bewitching. As I strained to follow it, a roar of stomping hooves rose from nowhere. A wild power swept through the forest, until just as suddenly the commotion stopped. The atmosphere felt thick and charged. A timorous voice, hoarse and shrill, urged me on from the shadows, "Keep going. Your place awaits you at the fire beside Great Mother Tree. Titania, Queen of the Elementals, will guide you into the realm beyond this one. She rules over the Plant People and their dominions, the Faerie, and the little folk, who once walked this Earth as visibly as you."

The fire glowed through the trees and crackled like gunfire. A circle of small people sat, and nodded approvingly at my arrival, some holding up their hands to the flames. At first glance, they looked nondescript, wearing the timeless uniform of cloaks, fur, skins and dark cloth. Their distinct profiles and heavily-set features became exaggerated in a comic play of light and shadow: lines like creases, noses and chins hooked or angular, eyes bright and clear, hair sprouting or tufty. All those gathered had the look of being children reared by the forest. Their age was hard to place – neither young nor old. I followed their gaze to a woman perched on the roots of a giant tree, the folds at its base framing her like a throne. Its trunk, the widest I'd ever seen, stretched upwards. The woman held the rapt attention of every man and woman present even though she was just as small. As I too stared on, her pretty face shone translucent and her hair was as black as the darkest night. A sparkling tiara offset her eyes radiant with lively wit and humour. Her lips were like pouting rubies in contrast with the dull animal fur slung about her neck, and green fabric draped around her, as fluorescent as moss.

She might have been half my size, but her authority could not be questioned. Her dark eyes pierced mine in welcome. Motioning an arm across the circle, she spoke out in a high singsong voice. "It has been some time since you last came this way. My subjects and I are, as you may remember, caretakers of the green kingdoms and their people held deep within the belly of the Earth."

I acknowledged everyone gathered, who gifted me warm smiles of welcome. Our encounter was expected. Queen Titania who had been watching me answered a rising flood of questions. "My people are as loyal to Mother Nature as every instinctual being would ever be. They have pledged to serve the balancing forces of every enchanting space until the end of time. Although we could have left this world as an exodus so many moons ago, we have sworn allegiance to every plant that has ever been so that it may always flourish. The Elementals hold crucibles of every spore and seed, long since extinct. Despite what you humans believe with your Darwinian logic, my people enjoy the earliest genus of plant and fern, algae and lichen, and nurture the chlorophyll and carbon of all green matter. Among the trees and all green places they can still be seen at play, by those of your kind with the keenest eye. More rarely, a few still venture into your towns and cities."

"But how can ancient nature be thriving from what you say, when it's extinct?"

Ignoring me, Queen Titania giggled. Clapping her hands excitedly, she pointed to a gap in the circle. That, she explained, had been held for me throughout time. It was my place, and had remained empty, guarded over by the Elementals, until the moment, this very one, I chose to reclaim it. I edged into the circle, aware of the friendly eyes returning mine. "Now, my sweet one," she continued, her voice deepening in seriousness. "It is all too clear you have forgotten the elemental magic in the land of your distant ancestors. They knew how much they needed us and so we lived united in common purpose. This Earth was a harmony once of peace and plenty. The ancient ones venerated every feature of the natural world as an inseparable part of their own living body. They understood the equality of all Mother Nature's creations – and respected us as her chosen stewards. It is true that without our cooperation, none could penetrate the depths of our Earth without getting lost or trapped along the way. You, it seems, have swallowed the false infor-mation, indoctrinations, the manipulative dogma and collective amnesia of your species. It is a falsehood to believe the Earth a solid ball of fire and crust!"

At this, a trill of laughter swept through the circle. I didn't feel in any way defensive for being laughed at. It felt uplifting being the object of jolly ridicule, as some doubled over, others wheezed, all gasping for breath between the next heave of laughter. Humour, being infectious, made everything suddenly very funny. Soon I too was laughing. Queen Titania had pointed out a mad twist of reason – the conjecture the Earth was a solid mass. How could I have been so gullible? Who were these experts, scientists, educators and know-alls anyway? A chain of memories came to me, of different classroom scenes, childhood moments, airplane journeys gawping at the marvels of the Earth's surface, outdoor trips pounding vast areas of terra firma, daydreams of exploring ocean depths and mountain ranges on the impene-trable seabed. Looking back on those assumptions with fresh knowingness, I saw how innocently I had swallowed standard accounts of the planet's history, regarding the facts within every textbook and journal, documentary and lecture the incontestable truth of official events. As the mirth settled down after a few false starts, I felt a tremendous kinship with my neighbours. When Queen Titania spoke again, there was a sudden hush as we all listened attentively once more.

"There are many entrances into the Earth that were once the everyday knowledge of birds, animals, insects and man. Now they are a closely guarded secret. We are their gatekeepers. Some are large gaps in the remote ice regions of the poles, volcano vents, others caves, secret passageways beneath ancient temples, the crevassed seabed and also burrows of our furry rodents. Mount Bugarach, as you discovered, is another. Only, all these openings are not what they might seem. They may look like a wild animal's shelter or a hole too small for a human to enter. Many such spaces open up further down, some miles below our ground, to become caverns and grottos and gaping tunnels, a labyrinthine network of paths and alleys leading deep into the womb of the Earth and beyond. That is how you reached us, following the tunnel here."

"But the Earth, it's always said, is filled with magma," I piped up. "Everyone knows molten lava and crust is at the heart of our... solid planet."

"No, my dear, that burning layer is nearer the surface than you think. Beyond that is space! The cooling and spinning of a planet ejected from a star or sun creates such hollowness. At the heart of the Earth, its nucleus, a globe of energy shines brilliant. It is like an inner sun, suspended by gravity and centrifugal force. It is the light of the aurora borealis. My dear, your heart longs to explore the vast spaces driven by the primal heartbeat of Mother Nature. Inside her belly are oceans where beings thrive in plankton rich waters. The interior is teeming with rich life: amphibians, lagoons and rainforests, roamed by the Earth's first reptiles, savage and deadly. There are exotic areas filled with ferns and plants predating trees. They feed on the milky-bright light of reflecting minerals. Whatever you have chosen to think, life persists everywhere, unstoppable! The Earth is brimming with life – indeed, it is more lush and radiant inside than out. You humans have swallowed the lies of your heritage!"

There was a murmur of agreement in the circle. I felt lucid and calm as Titania's words seeped through my awareness like smoky wisps. They felt as familiar as imprints of memory long forgotten. A drum began pounding beneath the soft chords of a lyre. The night was alive, every living thing awake. Melodies, soothing and gentle, guided me to insights and decisions. I had to venture into the Earth and see for myself the truth of what I had been told. Yet my everyday reason was as strong as this growing curiosity. As the music swept me up I could feel the rush of flowing water – snaking towards the Great Ocean far beyond. A white wake foaming on its every twist and turn lulled me into a cradle-like rock. I was back at the beginning. This was my carriage to the source of what needed remembering. It was a journey to discover what I called 'the world'.

The rock, boulder, pebble, stone, crust, canyon and ravine had been the first to weather the ravage of time and hostile storms which once raged unceasingly around the planet. Oh so slowly, the Plant People had sprung up everywhere turning the Earth green. They were sparks of primitive life, their cells programmed to develop organically, ripened by the moist warm climes. Trunks then emerged, so that the first plants could climb the skies, catalysed by another quantum step in nature's armoury. I glimpsed the unlikely and irrepressible miracle of life's evolution – how every cell harboured the potential for new worlds to mutate and diversify. Among the wild greens and exquisite flowers of the exotic primeval epoch, magical stone cathedrals housed their stewards: the Elementals, the lineage of Queen Titania. They were like armies of anthropomorphic ants singing songs to homage the marvel of Nature.

All life seemed ablaze with the excitement of unfolding, the discovery of all to come. Death flowed from life wherever it sprung – one step forwards, two back, together then apart. It was a dance without end, a precious alchemy of unforeseeable creations. What was this inexorable force, its power so persistent and fragile? Death trailed life, in a rhythm of tide and cycle, pulse and heartbeat, in-breath and out-breath, decay and bloom, drought and fertility, vitality and slumber, winter and summer, nights following day: endlessness without repetition. Each part in the story of creation needed its other face to counter it. Without opposites nothing could ever be.

"Tell me about this tree, Queen Titania," my voice echoed as in a dream.

"This sacred Mother Beech glints copper, as holy as the Oak, her consort. In what you humans call early civilisation, which in truth followed hundreds of thousands of years of growth and enterprise (now that's a case to revise your school curriculums!), the bark was stripped to become pages of the first books. Back then there were no words, only symbols and designs mirroring the building blocks of all life. This tree is venerated for its knowledge. It is a living library, a record of evolutionary wisdom."

Nothing grew near the tree. Its commanding presence demanded space and light. Its branches dwarfed treetops, from where a burst of song pealed out as thousands of tiny birds launched from their nests. The trunk was polished with patterns, simple almond-shaped markings all over the bark, reminding me of primeval fish or the all-seeing eye of Horus. Again, Egypt glimmered through the veils of time – its ancient imprint recognisable at once. There was a synergy at play: as I saw, so I was seen. At the point where the trunk split into branches, my eyes were drawn to a faint outline of two books. One looked filled with words, the other blank. The book with words, I knew, held the influences shaping my life. It represented the probable world of cause and effect. Its pages then opened up, as whole scores of musical notes streamed from them, emitting sound and tone. My heart began to race as feelings arose – sadness and joy, loss and laughter. I wanted to know what stories those pages held, what landscapes and people they evoked.

As I focused on a symbol, scenes would form, places not yet encountered in time. This book was a vibrant composition of trials and triumphs, with all the joys and regrets of a loving life well lived. I could sense lighter, lyrical passages within the whole and darker, stodgier ones, everything breaking up in a staccato of change. There was not much peace within the pages, but plenty of vital contrast and excitement. The more I stood back, the more beautiful those pages became. I liked this book. It held the promise of an extraordinary life, a creative laboratory to explore ideas, places and people. It wasn't a cosy read; its drama sure to liven up a dull day. The winters in it made the summer sun all the brighter and more nourishing.

My attention turned to the empty book. There were no colours or patterns, or anything identifiable within its pages. Nothing seemed to be held in them at all. As I waited, an unmistakable pulse began springing up through the pages like the faintest heartbeat. The book was coming to life! I felt the deep peace of certainty – with nothing in mind to be certain about. The book was a container of chaos and order without meaning. It held pure possibility. There was unimaginable power within the crisp blank pages. Everything and nothing. Both of equal value, as one and the same thing!

"Which do you choose?" A slow clear voice prompted me from within the tree's depths. It was a familiar voice, not yet encountered, from another time and place in my life. I recognised it at once. It was an echo of the dream to come – in which I met the Weaver – during one long night, so very far away – at Bugarach. She was to immortalise my untold story – that could only be claimed by stepping through the gap in time's flow. That time was to come – during an eclipse.

"You mean, which book?"

"Are you ready to rewrite your story?" her voice persisted.

"You mean, my life story?"

"Are you tired and dispirited enough, or even curious to

wonder what might happen if..." Her voice trailed into silence. I felt the long dark night opening up as though unzipped.

"If... what? What might happen?" I cried out, eager to listen on.

"You choose to dream up the truest story you could ever tell and live it so?"

"And then?"

"Which do you choose: the book that is written, or the one yet to be written and lived as it is told?"

I gazed at both, eager to snatch the first, the one documenting experiences I knew well and those to come. It charted the full story with all its formulaic ingredients that had led me to this point in time and my probable trajectory. Its familiarity had magnetism, making me want to curl up by a fire and bask at its warmth, a purring cat. But I knew I wanted the other more. The empty book. The book of blank pages, nothing in them – no story to shape a horizon or explain the terrain in between.

About to declare it, my throat was gripped by fear. A blank page – the crippling freedom of erasing the past! A new start without a hint of what to come! It was uncharted space – so easy to become lost in. One of the little people stood beside me, carrying a burning stick. Its cream-gold flare lit up the higher tree, from where a scroll unravelled to the forest floor. A sentence formed in the handwriting of a child.

"I am limited by all that has been and is to follow."

"This is a soul contract you made a long, long time ago," Queen Titania explained. "It is a little outdated. Like everything else, it has to be transformed for the new to emerge."

"But they're only words."

"Exactly," she replied with all the patience of a parent illuminating a bewildered child. "They hold beliefs in place which determine the course of events."

"But events happen anyway – they come and go."

"You determine events."

I thought back to the circle that Grandmother had halved – showing me how the hidden part of me had more power to create than I had realised.

"Some of them, of course," I conceded. "Clearly there are others over which I have no control."

"Oh just how clearly is that so?" Queen Titania retorted sweetly, despite an edge to her voice. "Which book do you choose? One charts life happening to you, the other for you. One presents the illusion of control, the other reflects whatever you are willing or ready to see."

Dimly I sensed an opportunity – a chance to slip through the doors of time to an unknown place, which wasn't a destination. "I'll choose the book with no words, as that is the route to meaning."

"The book is blank," Queen Titania reminded. "There is no written meaning within it or route to meaning. It holds no such promise."

"Then what is the point of that book?"

"There is no point. That is the point!" Again the circle laughed.

The little man beside me, clasping the fiery stick, patiently looked on at the dangling scroll that glowed with all the radiance of conviction. His dignity suggested his entire life had been in motion for this very moment, to assist me in whatever I choose to do. His round eyes blinked earnestly, as I reached for the torch he was holding. The scroll had to be burnt, for the freedom of choice to follow. One of its corners curled, the heat scorching the yellowed parchment black. The final words of the contract were the first to be blackened.

"I am limited by..." remained. The lingering words smouldered until they too were charred. Both books had disappeared. The trunk and branches looked ordinary, but for their size.

"What now?" I asked, turning instinctively to Queen Titania.

"You have chosen the blank book – it lives inside your heart.

Each moment from here on is meaningless until you declare it meaningful. You have reclaimed the power of your elemental heart, the soul of the journey you face – opening up to the bigger untold story to live through you. Your life is not your own; you are its instrument, as you face your death, which no amount of reason can explain away!"

Coached by Grandmother, encouraged by the spirit of the Elementals, recorded by the Weaver, I had to place myself in the ageless story of my brothers and sisters before – into the archetype of the lonely exile, forsaking the home so loved. I had to feel my way to passion, the only fuel that could inspire such a desperate choice to keep true to my heart: to risk losing every-thing – all those I loved, even my own life. I had to give up all ideas of safety and protection in the most heroic story I could tell. Tibet, for me now, was the domain of the unknown promised in the blank pages of the book I had chosen. There was no longer Queen Titania's kingdom taking life around me – only an impulse for the next step: over a threshold to face my deepest fear of the chilling loneliness in death.

Chapter 15

Exile in Tibet

The stars look so close you could touch them. The snow gleams. We lurch on through a frozen hell of black and white. There is no one but us. Those we've left behind are mostly forgotten. The mind has shut down, numbed. Each step, each heavy tread, is a burden to a dying body. Raising a leaden leg takes all the will a man can summon. Crunch. Crunch. Strange how alive my feet sound given I cannot feel them. The air is raw. It bites my lungs. My cheek throbs. Every time the wind gusts, unforgiving and savage, the face freezes. It is the price of our freedom. This is when I doubt, when my faith is most tested. More than by hunger, or losing the way, or never arriving.

Being numb is the biggest danger. At first, the senses are grateful. How sweet not to feel! The body was never made to withstand such deadening cold. The dark cold is inhuman. Two withering specks of life – childhood friends – persist against such odds. Angchuk and I have aged decades since leaving Lhasa. Without pain tethering us to life, our bodies will shut down in the end. Too tired and weak to fight the freeze those limbs of ours will give up.

The desire to sleep is so strong. We've barely stopped and already we have to get moving. The wall of ice guides us, luminous at night. It is in fact a treacherous guardian. Without it, we would be lost – but it creaks and sighs, as fragile as we are. It is no more solid than us. Tongues of frozen water move down the cratered wastes. How small we are against such forces! And still we labour on through the twisting ice.

How lonely it is tonight. Even the birds are sleeping, somewhere lower and warmer. They would starve too if they ventured to these heights. A shooting star sweeps across the vast sky, holding the secrets of which I understand little. What has brought me here? I cannot even turn round to Angchuk. He trudges far behind me. To look at him will speak to me of hopelessness.

What is that throbbing heat in my legs? Cold or fatigue? What now – when will this torture end? To give up, we will perish. To survive is too much to think of – refugees in a future of suffering and struggle. Carrying on, there can be no comfort either. Our jackets are as stiff as cardboard, mean and worn. From bursts of rest, we wake up crushed and empty. A dreamless void. Asleep or awake – our exile haunts us. The boots, the batons. How they stomp and strike, tormenting us, night and day. The invaders have destroyed our heritage, but not our soul. The heart of Tibet has been ripped open. To starve there would be worse than to perish here – cold, hungry but free? All we have we carry. What use is the bundle of notes, the paper savings, in this white wasteland? We must be near to others now as we near Nepal – to food, to warmth?

When we stop, we busy ourselves and eat. It is an effort to thaw some meat and 'tsampa', frozen like rock. When heat stirs within us, the spell of the past rises up again, invigorated, breathing life into our nightmares. We were cattle in Lhasa, not human beings. The hate on the faces of those bent on claiming our country: we were the parasites feeding off China's rightful land for a thousand years and more. Someone somewhere decided we were never meant to be there – that as Tibetans, we were squatters of Tibet. Our features might be just like theirs but the difference is we are undeserving. We are the wilful cattle, and respond to the voice of violence and submission.

The 1500-mile walk will take us to His Holiness. He will bless us and welcome us to refuge. Just months ago, he made this same journey by horse. It was warmer then. It was God's Grace, Divine Compassion that the Dalai Lama never endured this.

I stop to check Angchuk is following. Hunched, head bent, I

hear him panting, stumbling into the holes my boots have made. He starts to clap his hands together in the yak wool mittens lining his new gloves, made by nomads far below. Icicles sprout from his hat and jacket hood. Nothing can escape Winter's fingers and their icy grip. He stops still like an exhausted donkey. He doesn't look up at me but knowing I have stopped he stands mid-stride. A statue. We have to keep moving. It would take too long to thaw the remains of our last meal. Thirst now sears my throat. Eating snow is no good – it burns the mouth and shreds the tongue. We must move, eyes only on the snow in front. We have been lucky the snow bridges have not given way to the chasms they hide. Chance is watching over us. It will not abandon us. Like others before who survived, as we will, we are the torch of Tibet.

We cannot be far from the highest pass, the approach to Chomolangma, most hallowed peak of Mother Earth. The mighty mountain, the Jewel of the Himalayas, is our beacon. It is our gateway to liberty. Our omen. Only snow blindness or blizzard can stop us from beholding it. We will tie our Prayer Flags to the chink in these mountains, through which we will pass, beckoning us towards safety. There they will flutter and shred, returning to the earth as dust. Fragments of passing time. Is it two more days, three days, another week of this until the pass?

In the first light of dawn, my hope sometimes stirs from deep inside. That same feeling is awake in me now. The flurries of snow are really Heaven's dust. Each snowflake catches the new day, its yellow and crimson. When my eyelids are heavy or squint in the glare, the snow crystals become fireflies sweeping across a heavenly landscape. They flash a spectrum of colour, a magic capturing me between sleep and wakefulness.

Another gust whips though the gap in the buttress. It licks through my clothes, a crueller cold. The peace I've felt is only temporary, like all things. The light is bright green. There is menace in the beauty. This is like the poison of the most beautiful plants tempting man to eat them. It is a trap to catch him, to hold him prisoner, just when he is at his weakest, when he wants to believe in that most alluring to him. I must believe in the freedom ahead, where a new life waits for me. Surely I am not meant to doubt that dream now and see its treachery? Earth, I tell you, I cannot take any more cold!

Does she hear me? Her generosity is spent. No refuge in this wild exposure. Even its beauty is bleak. Indifferent, unyielding. We are ignored – or worse, forgotten. Is this the chill of exhaustion or dispossession? We are exiled – orphans of a lost nation, abandoned by our Mother Earth.

Where among the endless snowfields is my body now? Halfway there? No, this is only false hope. My toes are one stump of a tree. I am as naked and bare as a leafless poplar in winter. I am outside my body now. In all the blue whiteness, there is always the virgin green of barley in my memory. This is where my spirit lives. The soil in my fingernails, the smell of new growth as the yak furrow the field in fresh cycle. There is only silence in such labour, peace as the body works and mind stills. In that silence, only the Earth is to be found, the pulse of life's heart. Once, there was always food, always plenty. Earth offered its fruits tempering greed and want. I must keep going for Angchuk's sake, if not for my own! There will be peace again, a return to the way it must be, as it has always been for my people. One step. One more step.

Time stopped and I am still moving. Soon we will have another hazard. The glare of daylight brings fresh danger. It is not only the ravens that see us, swooping along the rocky ravines gouged by ice and time. Communist soldiers will be guarding the territories near the border. Nepal is some way ahead yet. But we must always be alert. Spies lurk. There is easy money to be made by whispering to the Chinese. Am I dreaming now but over there – how far, I do not know – I swear there is a flickering light. Stop now and ask Angchuk if he sees it too. If I stop I will freeze solid. One more step. One step. Two. Another. Move. Keep going. But there is a light. I know it now.

I stand back against a pane of thick ice and wait for my friend. The mountain is white, blue and grey at this height. Clusters of fresh snow are seared by the wind, their edges like airborne arrows. Or perhaps more like tiny birds, their feathers frozen? I am losing my mind. Still it – but not stop it dead. Angchuk keeps going. He is only ten feet away. Keep going my friend. I am here, watching you – do you see the light over there? That is food. That is shelter. Rest and warmth.

Eventually, he reaches me and slumps still, willing himself to look up. I touch his wooden shoulder but I need to keep my arms crossed, to shield my frozen self from more cold. I nod to the light. He looks over and stares. Without looking at me, he nods back. Neither of us have the energy to speak. During these long days and nights, we have said little. Both of us feel the other's private hell. Even that has to be shut out – not enough strength to bear the agony of your greatest friend too, your dearest brother. What now? Do we head over there, and what will we find? There could not be soldiers here, surely?

Some force wills us towards the light. As we move slowly on, it disappears in the thickening clouds. I swear I can see the face of my horse in the swirling grey. Dolma is staring at me, her nostrils gaping as she snorts. Her eyes are the two dark patches looking straight into mine. How many happy hours have we spent at work together, master and mule? One carries the other, or his loads to market, bearing his supplies from Lhasa, along the steep and narrow trails home. The whistle of the wind is almost like her whinny. Shall I point this out to Angchuk – will he recognise the vision too? The shape is changing fast. Her nose is there but the eyes are thinning. Already she has gone.

One step, then another. My feet don't mind the freezing damp now – they don't feel it. My heart doesn't care either – it is being drawn to the light and that is all that matters. One step. The snow has been waist deep in parts. Even chest deep. At least it is frozen here – we only drop two feet at a time. The light has gone out again, killed by daylight. A black shape is there instead. It is a blot of ink, staining the snow, changing shape with every step. Now it is frayed fabric. A loose thread unravelling. It is spinning a shape, though for the life of me, I don't know what. Does Angchuk see it too?

We are getting nearer. My nose is full of solid phlegm like stone. I cannot empty it because my fingers can't move. Breathing through my mouth makes me thirstier. I am spitting ice. My saliva freezes as it leaves me. When will I be warm and whole again? Angchuk is moving more slowly than before. I should wait for him but I have to keep moving. He must not disappear because I would never find the strength to look for him. Can he see that black patch, sheltered by overhanging rock? Reaching it is the only thing in the world we must do. Angchuk moves as he will in old age, bent and frail. For one so strong with life, he is nothing but a shadow of himself. He only sees my track in front of him. That is his horizon now – an endless trail, promising safety, leading him into the mouth of a hostile wind.

Listen to its howl now. Over the pass it will be a rattle, only matched in fury by death's sudden lunge. After any storm, there is peace, but never soon enough. We have lost much weight and our clothes are looser. To abandon any more of our precious kit won't make us lighter. We will still sink through the snow. The extra socks, hat and blankets may be our curse at times, but they are our salvation when we stop to sleep. Ice is the most unwelcoming bed to an exhausted man. How tired we must be to sleep even for short spells! I must will myself towards the black.

It cannot be more than thirty feet. That was my thought a long time ago, how long, I do not know – a block of time measurable by icy degrees. That is the only shape to be found in this white hell. My hunger does not matter. Nothing matters except the cold. Does the black have eyes? Is it human, animal? Is it mirage? Is it shelter? Yes, we have walked so far, we can reach it soon enough. Forty feet – yes, just a hundred more strides? Two hundred at most, short-nothing in the scale of what we have already endured. Try not to spit. I am thirsty and my empty stomach is eating itself, my spit its bile. I only want to reach the black. That is all that matters. Reaching the –

It is a flapping strip of material and animal skin. It must be the Drokpas. They are miles off their course – why this height in winter? Angchuk, keep going, my Angchuk. Warm tea will thaw our worn bodies soon. The shelter looks as if it will take off in the wind, whipping the forlorn threads that anchor it in the snow. This humble effort at taming nature will be blown away, leaving no human trace in the alien whiteness where man should not be. Tucked beneath rock, it is a palace compared to the jutting slabs that have housed us too often. There must be a mule or two, somewhere – how could they carry their needs otherwise? Surely no animal could survive this? I am too exhausted to care. The cold stings my face but it is free of the icy spume that tears the skin.

Angchuk is still there, barely moving from this distance. The gap between us has widened. He cannot get lost now. All he must do is keep to my tracks a little longer, that's all. I can't watch over you, Angchuk, when I am this close to warmth. I need to get there too, make our presence felt, introduce ourselves to the generosity of Chance. We have to get out of this wind.

"Hello?" My voice is hoarse, whiny. It won't be heard in this wind, no matter how much it has calmed. I kick at its opening – a tear, sealed by more fabric – and something hard as metal. Nothing. No reaction can be quick enough and so I kick again. Something moves at last. Slowly the layers are peeling away – there is life behind this door and it is working to welcome me inside.

Who is more surprised – me, or the weathered face in fur staring back through his hole, like a rodent caught by surprise. There is nothing to say except move through the fold of flapping cloth to warmth. The man understands this and shuffles aside. He is on his haunches and slaps my back as I crawl in, balancing my weight on my hands, kicking each raised leg free of snow outside, one at a time. I don't turn round as he seals the door again.

All I see is a big pot, with a cloud of steam pouring out of the crescent from an unclosed lid. A woman is cradling a small boy as she tries to fit it properly and seal in the heat. The lid must be bent or something because she grabs a metal plate from the floor and places it over the stubborn gap. A baby is bundled in a woollen shawl tied around the woman's neck. The child, its brother, stands up and pokes it, as if trying to rouse a lifeless pet from sleep. The mother doesn't seem to notice. Next to them, an old man is huddled in a threadbare blanket, emaciated and frail. They all look at me with half-dead eyes.

The boy is the most curious and frowns, apparently deciding whether the appearance of a visitor is real or not. He is thin and his cheeks covered in scabs from the sun that glares off the snow like fire. The old man has the deepest eye sockets I've ever seen – apart from the skulls of yak and goat littering the land near my family's farm. His face is so gaunt, he looks haunted, barely alive. The floor is a frayed straw mat. It is warmer than outside, but the conditions in here are as bleak as our own sorry state – which reminds me, where is Angchuk?

I look behind at the door. The man who let me in is no longer there. He must be outside helping Angchuk. There is no need to worry now and so I say a few words pointing to the pot: "cold", "food" and "tea". I try to smile by way of greeting but my face is about to crack. These words are so bare – nothing but the urgent truth. I try to soften my eyes like a pleading beggar – these people are not here for my survival. We are exiles and equally desperate.

The woman answers as her boy stares at me. Her accent is strong, from another region, but she is Tibetan. She nudges him to pick up a tin mug at the back of the tent. He empties it of snow and hands it to his mother before stretching his arms above his head despite the tent's sagging frame forcing the rest of us to sit. She lifts the plate and scoops the mug into the butter tea. It dribbles down one side as she hands it to me. I know I am being watched as I blow and sip it, my face in its steaming warmth. Never has tea been this good – its salt is the perfect medicine my body needs, its buttery surface the most nourishment in too long; numbed by snow, edging along steep, slippery rock, tormented and frail. My heart is the first part of this stiff worn body to respond. It is like Angchuk's family's cat only purring very faintly, long after the first stroke. Yes, my heart is stirring in the unfamiliar warmth spreading across my chest. Waking up from the dead.

The old man remains lost in himself and the mother rocks her baby. Only the boy sees me. Sometimes he turns to his mother and puts a gloved hand on her lap but she does not respond, except to look down every now and then at her sleeping baby. I cannot see its face, cocooned by wool. We are all too weary to find out how we have been brought together like this, what has made us venture across the frozen wilds in the thin icy air of winter. It hardly matters but the tea is warming my blunted mind.

A draught bores into my back and I picture it making a hollow. The tent door is starting to flap as its outer part is opened first. It is Angchuk being helped through. His jacket is white with snow and fine icicles cling to his hood. His eyes are like creases, swallowed by tiredness and cold. His face is puffy and red sore. He is too numb to notice as I shuffle aside to let him sit, holding his arm to show his friend is at his side again. He is no longer Angchuk but a block of ice. The man who helped us in has finished fiddling with the door and looks around for something. He sees the plate on top of the pot and places it against the door's corner, then thinks better of it and stuffs a bit of rag from his pocket there first. Heat is precious little even in here and every fine crack or tear its enemy.

At last he stares at the two strangers, apparitions from the gloom. The cold is seeping into my bottom and so I change position and sit on my haunches as the man is doing. The old man has barely stirred; his empty eyes are in a different world. The man claps his hands together to feel some life, and tells his wife to serve more tea. She hesitates and looks straight at him, as if to question the wisdom of this. There is scarcely enough for them but when she glances at Angchuk, she must understand that to deny him tea could kill him. Again she speaks in that funny dialect to the boy, who hurries over to the only other cup I can see, anxious to please her.

I put my arm round Angchuk and hold the tea for him. I blow on it while his dull eyes blink at its steam.

"Drink," I tell him.

Slowly, with great effort, he bends his whole body in one lowering motion, one inch, maybe two, as I lift the cup to his bloodied lips.

"Take this, Angchuk."

He can't open his mouth, which is chapped and cracked like the weathered rocks outside. "Drink," I command.

This he hears because at last his lips open as I tilt the cup very carefully. Some slurps down his chin before he remembers to shut his mouth and swallow.

"More. Take more."

It is like operating a puppet that will only function if the right strings are pulled. We are bound in a new relationship – am I a father now to my friend? The drink is his lifeline. How fragile life is, held by the breath, the continuity of each single breath.

I pause between each sip to allow the warmth to seep through him. It will take time. To drink too much might overbear his weary body. At last he flinches, as if expecting the next sip. This block is warming up. It has memory. Yes, there is life in Angchuk yet, the playful prankster of our childhood. He was the master who built our perfectly constructed hideaways, and I his willing assistant. With the skills of a magician, his beautiful dens would arise from discarded mud bricks and rusting, rotting waste. He would plan the designs, as well as our stealth to obtain building tools. We stole a spade one night from a landowning neighbour. How we treasured that carved handle, and curved blade that spoke of real men, real work – the trouble we took burying it. Where would it be now? No value here, heavy and still too small to be of any use in the unending snow.

That's it, my friend. His feeble sips remind me of that mewing, scrawny cat he loved so much. His eyes are roaming a little as life returns to them. Angchuk takes the cup now and his eyes rest on the greasy pools of the tea. I turn my attention to the draughts chilling the cramped space. It would be colder still outside. Fine shards of ice hang from the canvas above our heads. It is silent except for the wind. These people are stone still. Are they stopping themselves from drinking the tea to make it last? The man is waiting for us to warm. What is the rush for words? He ignores the boy who is pulling at his sleeve. How endlessly flat and grey this world of cold would be to a child. The wind is louder. The calm during the night was a false serenity. It sounds like a front is coming in. The tent is flapping with urgency.

The man tells his wife to fill Angchuk's cup a second time. I think I should refuse for him – he is still too gone to notice the enormous sacrifice these people are making for us, every bit as desperate as we are. But one look at Angchuk tells me to keep quiet. He needs more tea.

The wind is building all the time. A storm. The child looks unafraid, perhaps used to the weather's violence, or more likely, unaware of its danger. I try to take the cup from Angchuk to help him drink so that he may revive more quickly. He shakes his head, the surest sign yet he is back inside his rigid body. I see his cup has been filled less than half full this time. Without my help he slowly takes a sip. The man then catches my eye as I study his alert face, wondering if he too senses a storm. Even if Angchuk does recover his strength, we would be lucky to last the night if we head out in this weight of wind.

The old man must be close to death. There is no spare flesh left on him. Wattles of skin hang from his chin like the loose lobes of a turkey's neck. Can he really last another day? The mother holds the baby stiffly. How quietly it sleeps. Her son is wrapping a tattered piece of cloth round one hand, with all the solemnity of a Lama preparing incense. He notices me watching him and, clearly unused to attention, starts to make a performance of this mindless act. He checks again and again that I am still watching, and tries to give me his best smile before turning his eyes to the rag. I am too tired to play this game but I know this is what he needs. He is only four or five and playing is what we do in those early years of life.

Angchuk bends over his cup again and puts all his effort into tipping it. The doorway is being shaken up by the wind. The man is aware of the worsening weather now, the others too half-dead to notice. The folds of the tent at the entrance are whipping his back and so he gets up and starts working at the door. He will need my help to secure the tent and make it fast. Sensing this, he turns round and nods at me and I crawl out behind him. From outside, he points to the plate put to one side of the door, next to Angchuk. I also grab another. They will be useful spades for digging at the new snow. If it blows harder, we will need to take it in turns working for the rest of the day, or the tent will get buried like a grave.

Thick snow is tumbling out of the sky. The peaks have disappeared. It is impossible to tell where the sky meets the ground. We start to scrape away the fresh snow from one side of the tent. The wind has no clear direction. The tent ought to be side-on, but the gale is not settling and the others would have to come outside if we moved it. Instead, we dig a trench and stack the piles of snow into a makeshift wall. We will have to work every hour, so our shelter will get bigger. At least that will keep us warm and occupy our minds to keep fear away.

It is too cold to carry on. We both make for the door. He insists I go in first; to carry on shaking my head would ensure we freeze. It is impossible to stop the snow from following us in. We try as best we can to shovel it out. Nothing has changed inside. Angchuk is bent over his tea, the mother clasps her baby and the old man is looking blankly at his feet. Only the child is alert staring at us from his frozen perch beside his mother. I nod at the man and then the tea, urging him to drink. He misunderstands and offers me some. "No, you," I say. "You have the tea." He tells his wife to drink but she doesn't seem to hear and continues to look lifelessly at the rumpled woollen cradle of her lap. The baby has been miraculously silent, in blissful slumber, innocent oblivion.

At last the man takes a cup for himself. While he sips, I gesture to the old man that he should have some too. But he doesn't see me. "No," is the clear answer back. "He is waiting for death." At last our histories will unite – sharing how we came to meet in this hell.

"Has it been very difficult?" I ask.

"More difficult than we could ever have imagined. We left east, Kham, much later than we wanted. There was too much to do. In the end we abandoned everything. But that would not have changed anything."

"This – " he points vaguely upwards at the formless savagery of winter.

"This is surely the coldest winter ever known," I finish his sentence for him.

Angchuk must have drunk all his tea, yet he tilts his cup to his lips now and then and swallows every last drip like a bird. The boy is not interested in the nourishing butter tea, but holds his gaze on the two strangers instead.

"We lost our horse early on. He became so weak. He just

collapsed – that was it. We were going to sell him before getting any higher. That was the idea. Now we have no money. No papers. We don't know who to trust in Nepal."

"What are you carrying?"

"Everything you see. We have some salt. We hope to sell it and make something when we reach Nepal. But it is heavy. I have to carry it. My wife – " he gives her a desperate look, resting his eyes on her immobile face, "she has – my son to carry." I look over at the woollen baby, its face still hidden.

"So, your other son, he – walks as well?"

"No. As I say, he has to be carried." Yes, to walk would be impossible for a child that size. It would vanish in the sinking snow like a stone in water, his little body ravaged by cold. Within an hour, he would surely be dead. "My father has not long left," he continues. "He was old when we started but – he is much older now. He feels he is a burden to us, that we will all perish if he stays. He knows his time on Earth is ending."

"He is choosing to die, here?"

"Yes."

"How will you – " I stop myself. The cold is making me loose tongued. They will not have the means to cremate his body – that is obvious. It will be thrown into a crevasse, where it will rest preserved in its icy tomb, outliving its descendants. We return to the silence of our thoughts and the howling wind. One of the icicles is twisted like fraying yarn. A bubble of air is trapped in its centre, perfectly delicate and vital. It is reminding me to keep present to the countless tiny miracles that can revive shattered spirits.

"It will be so hard without him. He is my best friend. I have learnt so much from his knowledge."

There is nothing I can say to this, except feel this man's despair. At least Angchuk and I have only ourselves to consider. I look again at the man's father, who is not listening to us. He is too far gone. The wife is barely here either. She will need to draw on her every reserve of strength and love to keep her children alive. Angchuk stirs for the first time from his tea. "Angchuk? How are you, my friend?" At last he looks at me and something of him returns. He tries to smile – but only his eyes can do that. "Thank you," he says to no one in particular.

"Big wind," I point out needlessly. "We will have to wait until it blows itself out."

"Yes," Angchuk says and then looks at the man. "And you? Will you stay?"

"How long, who knows? One day, two more days. No more than that – or we will never leave. We have little to eat – some *tsampa*, butter and horsemeat. Much of that we have thrown away – it is too heavy. We lost our rice after it got buried one night in the snow."

"We have some sugar to give you, maybe more *tsampa* too," I say, knowing how little we have ourselves. The child curls into a little ball and its head rests against his mother's knee for a pillow. She does not touch him or look at him. "We could cook something together? Mix some meat and *tsampa*? A spoon of sugar too?"

No one hears me. It is time to shovel the snow. Again, the man senses what I am thinking, and as before, we rise at the same time and crawl out into the whirling white, one after the other. We dig as quickly as we can, pack the scooped snow against the wall and return to the refuge of the tent.

Angchuk is looking better and says he will cook. It is no longer a question of delay. All of us must eat. Our strength depends on it. He reaches for one of our packs and empties the extra gloves, socks and blanket, his ration of *tsampa* wrapped inside. I tell him to find the charcoal in the other pack. It will take an age to thaw the food and melt the snow to make a stew and so I shut my eyes. Only now the tiredness I have been fighting overwhelms me. Waves of exhaustion swamp my battered body. It is my turn to become dead and return once more to the void of sleep. Once or twice I force myself to stir and look up at Angchuk to see if the food is ready. He remains hunched over the blocks of ice, waiting patiently for the modest stove to melt them into something we can eat.

An hour passes, maybe two. I am sure the tent is flapping with less violence when I wake up. Angchuk is stirring the pot, now steaming. The man must be outside. The boy sleeps and so does his mother, still cross-legged but with her head slumped forwards. The old man has not moved but is less visible somehow. I swear he is dissolving. I pat Angchuk's back and pick up the plate sealing in the warmth from the pot's uneven lid. This will be my shovel again.

Outside, the man is working at the wall. The storm is less angry and the snow is not falling in sheets like before. I begin to pat the other end from where he is, reinforcing the sides with extra snow. Eventually we meet near the middle and stand back to assess our protection. This will last the night. The light is fading. It must be close to early evening. Just as we are about to head back into the tent, I touch the man's arm to point out the omen smiling over us. An aura of light is piercing the gloom, its edges an electric gold. As we watch, a small rainbow sphere bursts through it. A miracle of light in the gloom! Each moment is thrilling to watch as it fades, briefly staining the patch of grey sky red, then the deeper crimson of a bloody scratch. The light is yellowing now; it will be dark within the hour. It is sure to be a better day tomorrow. We head to the tent where our first meal in two days waits for us.

We eat in silence, the man, the woman, the child, Angchuk and me. The meat is stringy and crunchy where it has not thawed – but the salt in it is good. The *tsampa* tastes as it usually does but I notice Angchuk has added some butter, a special touch for such a long way from home. It is quite warm and that is the main thing. The old man is worrying me. There is hardly any spare room but even lying down he does not fill any space, a ragged bag of bones he has become. "Your father must drink some tea," I say to the man.

Without answering, he scoops some into a cup and leans over the old man who must be asleep. His scrawny frame, like a birdcage, rises and falls with each deep breath. The man wakes his father up and then cradles his limp, frail body against his lap with one arm while holding the cup to his lips with his other hand. The old man blinks with the effort of taking some and then splutters. He cannot have swallowed anything for hours. Warm liquid trails out of his mouth. He cannot be so far gone – because he is trying to keep it in, but he coughs spraying the rest over his chest.

I look down at my bowl and will myself to eat the strange stew. It is barely warm but it is fuel to help us on our long trudge in the morning. Angchuk is struggling too. He is swirling the meat around with his finger. The old man is once again asleep. His son swills back the remains of the cup and returns to the only spare space. We sit, each of us working at the food we know must be eaten. The woman laboured over her smaller portion, her hand rising and falling from her mouth in continuous motion until it was finished. Her son whispers to her and she tells him to eat up the last morsel. His plate now empty, he leans against her but her arms remained wrapped round her bundle. The baby must have only been fed when I had been outside, sparing my frayed nerves from its cry.

The three of us finish our food and sleep beckons at once. The wind has calmed but we must ensure the trench around the tent is cleared of any new snow. Angchuk moves to follow us but I tell him not to worry. The man and I know what to do. It is no longer snowing and after we have finished, we look up at one lone star peeping through cloud. We return inside and my only concern is to abandon myself to sleep beside Angchuk, who is curled like a ball in a corner.

I wake with a start a few times to darkness. It is cold and I huddle closely around Angchuk, pulling the blanket we share tighter around my back. Despite the long moments between sleep, time passes because at last it is lighter. I can barely hear the wind but it is surely all the colder for its stillness. My first thought is to rouse and get moving. The storm is over, but I feel new anxiety. Angchuk stirs too and the man watches us, already sitting, his arms wrapped around his bent knees. There is no life in the rest of the tent. He must have already been outside because his jacket is doused in a fine coat of wind-carried snow.

"How is it outside?"

"It is fresh for sure. But clearer," he says.

I am about to say something about pressing on once the weather settles. My instinct screams at me to get going without delay. This is a death trap. The atmosphere is bleaker in this damp space of shelter than the raw outside. The man urges us to have some tea and he gets working with the stove. Angchuk and I wait as he labours over the pot, in this final act of friendship. The boy wakes and gazes at his father from his thinning quilt. His eyes are older than they should be for one so young. He senses how he has to remain quiet, invisible for his parents' sake.

We sip the butter tea in the only two cups. I try to share mine with the man but he refuses. I am much warmer now than yesterday when we arrived, because my heart is bursting with an overwhelming sadness. It understands tragedy is lurking here. Death is life's key, liberating it to a dimension no humble human mind can grasp. Yet some other loss is hovering like a shadow.

"Is there anything we can do for you?" I ask him, desperate to give away anything he wants. He sits silently, his eyes in some far away place. The man within him is so alone. We finish our tea and at last he answers.

"We are cursed... our family and neighbours told us to wait until the thaw of spring. Again and again they urged us not to move just yet... to wait longer. But I was deaf. My eyes were the witness of Tibet sinking. I could not bear our people's misery, our rights stolen, living without hope day after day. We could have waited but summer has its own dangers. And so we went... and we have lost everything."

"Please," I urge, "we will leave you whatever food we can spare. You have saved our lives. There must be something we can do – we can help you move, help carry your load."

"Death is the heaviest load."

"Your father has lived long, he – "

He interrupts me, his voice clear and firm. "We have lost our little boy."

"No. He is fit and strong. Thin, yes. But he is very much alive." To prove the point, I look over to him, to his curled up resting body. His eyes meet mine – always alert, never missing anything. The man says nothing. I smile at the boy. His face tries to move but he gives up. How sad he is.

Remembering Angchuk and the long day ahead, I nudge him and nod at the packs. He starts to gather the blanket still wrapped around our legs. As sudden as a thunderbolt, the terrible truth of their misery strikes me. Their hopelessness is overwhelming. I wonder at the state of my mind. I can only gaze in horror at the sleeping woman's back. How quiet her baby has been. Disturbingly quiet. No baby can rest like that, even when sated with food and warmth. Oh, dear God, help these people, this is too much, this is not the natural order! The baby was born to live, not die within a hair's breath of life's unfolding. I think back to the mother's mute embrace. Of course, it is no wonder she cannot let go of her baby as she clings to the illusion she will wake from her coldest nightmare.

"Please. We must help you," I implore. But the man isn't hearing me now. Angchuk understands. We look at each other and, at once, begin to pack our sacks – what else is there we can do? There is no word to convey the depths of this family's grief, their lonely horror. "Please?" I repeat, like a whining child, grabbing the man's frozen sleeve. He takes my hand and I look into his empty eyes – what are they seeing?

"You must both get going," he says and then reaches out for Angchuk's hand and holds it too. Like a chain, the three of us sit together, our hands clasped. "God bless you both. We will always be Tibetans."

Through the flap for the last time, we crawl out. We will have to retrace our way along this vast snowfield to the col and cross into the next valley. I lead the way – and it is a relief to work against the snow in which our bodies sink, each stride inching us further from that sorry family. I know the relief is false. Like the threads that spin and forever bind us to all those we encounter, our hearts will always carry that family's burden. Down I go, chest-deep. It will take hours to cross the snowfield. The climb ahead will be easier – icier from being exposed to the wind. I am grateful though for the effort. Angchuk's mind will also be occupied with our exhausting struggle. But of course, this is only a reprieve. The memory of their kindness, sharing everything they had left in the world, will always haunt me, like Tibet, its spirit for now a guttering candle.

I only stop for breath and turn after we have moved some distance. At first I cannot see the tent. Its black fabric blends into the rock too sheer for the snow to hold. For a moment I allow myself to wonder if those desolate wanderers were the ghosts of a dream. Then, the tattered canvas shelter is there once more. Nothing moves. Only a heavy silence seems to separate our own sorry prospects from theirs. Vessels of ebbing life in all this bleakness.

Chapter 16

On the Wing

They glide with a grace and hover with a poise that defies gravity. The big birds are magnificent and powerful. Watching them inspires me. I yearn to experience their majesty of the skies. For such ease of flight, there is no density. Even when they dive to their prey, the air's resistance against their wings sharpens predatory instinct, making a swoop more deadly. A journey round life's wheel, as it approaches the airy realm of the East, also becomes more airborne. It is only inevitable. To jettison the baggage that amasses along the way in the grit of Time's trials is a freedom to be chosen. No luck can steady those wings. It is a skill honed from much practice.

The more complex a story, as a labyrinth of cause and effect, the denser it feels. Its spell lasts longer. It can wound like a curse or work as a mirror, with distortions more compelling than the sense to see through them. To change perception changes life itself. The storyteller cannot be separated from the tale they spin. As they undergo an initiation at every direction, from the South to the East, they grow noticeably lighter of load and emptier of narrative. Each gateway inspires a new perspective and in turn changes the world beheld.

Their cargo has been through the transformative heat of fire, under the sun's fierce glare at its South zenith. Purified in the flames of potential, their rage smoulders in the watery worlds harboured in the West. There they plunge into the charged realms of emotions and their stories thriving from deep underground. Unnoticed in the murky depths of the unconscious, they have sabotaged any chance of lasting joy. Facing their shadows is not enough. The journey demands the ultimate medicine of the West's gateway – lying far beyond the realms of death it guards.

Only when death is truly accepted can renewal follow. In the North, a bigger story starts to express as an archetypal impulse. A story has risen into collective territory far above the personal. It is here, among the Earth's mountainous vistas and icy wastes, that the fruits of rebirth take life, their medicine claimed. Choosing to step into the unknown invites the transformation the North promises. Only with this conscious sacrifice of the familiar and the rationale that had created the routine world can a brighter, more heart-centred story be lived. Life has elevated from mundane to epic. The realm of the North is where we encounter our Ancestors and their wisdom. Those before us and those to come are guardians of the Earth and its density.

It is when we approach the East that we remember our rightful place as Gods. Here is where the sun rises and life emerges renewed. This is the direction of unending potential, the pure possibility of light. As a place of resurrection, joy and fun is to be had soaring wing-to-wing with the elements of creation. This is not a place of escape, rather an integration of all there can be. It is in this state of possibility where we reclaim our wings, as free as air.

Far below are the valley's undulations. If the spirited heights are lofty and light, then the creased territories beneath are darker and contracted. They are recesses of soul – the grooves and folds a force field of gravity, pulling life downward to explore its terrestrial dimension. Descent is an invitation into the sensuous fruits of physicality – the rich here-and-now intelligence of a densely feeling nature. Such sensitivity is the gift and burden of being human.

One day, I came to understand that, to know it fully for myself. Nature, ever the best guide, showed me. I was wandering up a track between a tangle of hedgerows and ancient oak, gnarled and stooped by their exposure to the wild weather of Cornwall's north coastline. I could still hear the crashing waves of the Atlantic against fortressed rock walls – too high for scrambling down to the foaming sands. I had been edging along the cliffs. From where I had tried to find a route to the beach, a trio of climbers scaling the far wall opposite resembled ants. Frustrated, I pressed on inland, eager to discover what else this rugged coastline offered a stranger. It was right then, from the East, a hawk dipped and circled into view. Gliding to a standstill it hovered effortlessly – lording about the sky. Everything else faded out in the long moment of marvel, as I imagined myself beside that master of flight. A second hawk swept across the horizon to join it. Enthralled I watched their courtship unfold before me. I'd never seen the union among big birds – and never imagined how it might look as they fly. Their mating was a dance of the skies, with all the recognisable tricks of dating – coming together, swooping apart, rejoining. What followed was surprising. All of a sudden, they both plunged. Down they went, side-by-side, wing tips touching, outstretched and magnificent. Hundreds of feet they fell with all the urgency of survival. At such speed, a hawk looks like a kamikaze, diving to Earth for its assured suicide.

Being in love for these raptors is to fall in love, quite literally. Mating on the wing is a free fall of ultimate trust. It is poetic descent, when life and death conjoin. It is in this reckless instinctual act that inspiration and touchdown unite. Freedom is giving up the illusion there is another way. It is a flight of trust in life's supreme power. These birds demonstrate how mastery of physical laws and control are not the same thing. Nature abandons to gravity, tumbling to the Earth from the apex of flight in the only way it knows how.

This vision of everyday nature, so ordinary in its necessity, is extraordinary to witness. The union promised in death-embracing descent is also the trajectory I now choose to trust. It is when life's unstoppable force can be realised – felt in all its stupefying mystery.

In this part of my story, I book a last minute flight to Egypt. Its ancient mythologies unite the duality of existence, the worlds of sky and Earth. For many thousands of years, the supremely powerful civilisation was crowned by a hawk God – the lord of the skies, Horus. Also a falcon, he embodied human form as Pharaoh. The all-seeing eye of Horus roved the empire's towering wonders – its countless temples and the desert, mountains, river and coast. There was nowhere in the whole kingdom where Horus was not. As guardian, he watched over the grand drama of invincibility and decline, the rise and fall of imperial fortune.

To my imagination, Egypt crosses time, place and culture, as an ancient birth canal of the modern human story. In its overwhelming testament to the power of the past, I feel part of something much larger – an emerging era. I want to discover what lies beyond the content of the past, journeying down through it to the other side. What happens, I wonder, when those once critical stories have become so finely metabolised that they are at last a seamless weave of being? How does it feel no longer being identified with history or future – and not become detached or inhuman? The journey to an open heart doesn't bypass descent. Compassion, I'm sure of it, cannot be found in the lofty heights above human drama, but in grittier streets and darker valleys; a simple recognition of the challenge and suffering for so many others.

For all Egypt's audacious history, the desert as a fathomless marvel inspires me most. That is where I have chosen to stay. Its spaciousness makes me feel everywhere and nowhere at once. The stars of unending night skies bend the parameters of my everyday vision. They mirror another ageless map told in the desert sands; their subtle imprints like whispers to guide the roaming desert dweller, the terrestrial bird within us all.

Drifting off to sleep in my hotel in the Sinai desert, I listen to gentle waves washing over a sandy beach – that sing to me of migration and its unrest. Is the 'twinge' that has hounded me most of my life the same as the collective longing for a new song? I strain to hear the faint pulse of the night sky with all its stars, the mirror of a pathless journey far below. Oh the freedom to be a wanderer on this beautiful planet, for all its challenge! This is for now my dream, my song lulling me into deep restful slumber.

Chapter 17

Hatched Egg at Sinai

Well before dawn I rise with the call to prayer. Hauntingly melodic, some notes are perfectly discordant within its bigger harmony. It is not what is being sung, rather the quality of the naked voice itself, as a timeless instrument of devotion. At the edge of wakefulness, my imagination can glide into the fresh dream of a new day. There is a stillness to be relished as others sleep. Time seems to stretch making it easier to write. A tension drives me as the flow usually slows down when it gets light. My desk faces east on the veranda for when the sun rises. Mountains reappear in Ra's first rays, and the blue-silvered sea beneath them. My hotel is in a perfectly amphibious setting. The beach-front gardens are filled with man-made lagoons. As it gets lighter, they resemble blue kidneys against Sinai's parched desertscape.

During most daytime hours, I labour away on my manuscript. Each feeling stirred up within each story has been necessary to evoke as a stepping stone to its acceptance. Resurrecting the gritty months in the Amazon, as I have been recording them, has been uncomfortable. Even when I stop for the day, the jungle lives on an enervating presence. I understand Grandmother's challenge: the buried ghosts of my unexpressed regret and anger have to be felt for their exorcism. Only then can they be welcomed back home in my growing library of selves. Otherwise, they will continue to stalk from the shadows, and hijack my contentment from their hiding place. Avoiding our confrontation does not work forever. There is no enduring peace to be reaped in partial transformation.

I now know such denial was the cause of my twinge; Grandmother's very signature, her command to wake up and feel, as she raked over the flimsy foundations I tried to build, layered upon restless ghosts. Writing this book has invited their exposure, which has been reflected in everything around me. In the last few days, the desert has been lashed with hailstones and snow. The heaviest rainfall in decades has churned up sections of the airport road into impassable rubble islands – and how willingly would I stay marooned here! I had to come back to Egypt. It's under my skin. Its ancient lands make me nostalgic for something beyond the reach of memory. It is a place of mythic power, of Gods and Goddesses, self-determination, arrogance and blind courage. I could feel the magnetism of Sinai within the grey damp chill of Bristol winter. I listened, took note and arrived within weeks of its summons. My skin yearned sun, even a low sky winter sun. Sinai is the fabled desert in the Bible's book of Exodus, in which God appeared as the burning bush and Moses gifted the Ten Commandments. Enshrined in Christian lore, buses of tourists and pilgrims pay witness to the region's enduring power. I am also drawn to stories seamed within the desert – but not for their religious significance.

I can imagine the Weaver who inspired me to unthread my own life story, unravelling an older cultural drama, one that underpins everyday morality. The Old Testament's laws, all ten enshrined in sound sense, how might they be redrawn in a new age hurtling along the evolutionary timeline? For myself, I want to give up all rules – tear up the patterns and 'shoulds' of my life. I yearn for a blank script with all its unknowns. I can hear Grandmother declare in her no-nonsense manner, "We are born not to inherit, but to create! All that is no longer true must die along the way!" On my deathbed, with the precious clarity of a backward glance, what would become my ten commandments for full-blooded living? Who would I choose to become?

Wasn't that desire to set new rules behind the current turbulence in Egypt – the centre of the Arab Spring? Triggering unrest across the region, the uprising was rooted in outrage over oppressive governance. The call for empowerment has unbreakable momentum, to stall the power of history and rewrite the future. The oasis where I am based masks a lurking disorder. Seven years before, three bombs had shattered the peace of nearby Dahab, killing twenty-three people. The work of a lone terrorist is etched not only in memory, but in the town's stalled promise. A ghostly vision of prosperity is in the bulb-less lights along the town's snaking promenade. Shells of unfinished hotels were to host the sun-seekers and divers who never came. Elaborately carved, varnished signs are beside empty car parks and restaurants promoting huge discounts. Transforming the Bedouin beach settlement into a thriving alternative to the brash mass tourism of Sharm is unlikely to happen any time soon. Still, whatever its crumbling infrastructure and visible security presence, Dahab is a world away from the instability erupting elsewhere.

The international news channels have led for days on end with the chaos of riots in Port Said. Tahrir Square in Cairo is the other flashpoint and barometer of national rage. It doesn't surprise me Egypt is at the centre of regional uncertainty. The call for change is deeper than that rooted in half-baked dreams or passing discontent. Democracy has demanded bloodletting. Disenchantment set in for the elected Mahmoud Abbas and military echoes of his government. He has gone – and now a grim vacuum tails the revolution of old order. No one knows what is ahead – if anything, nothing has really moved on. A shake of the head, dulled eyes; wages are low, tourism is down, the police are corrupt. Freedom is tolerated only up to a very controlled point. There is work – toil and struggle, and more of that besides, to build any prospect of sustainable peace, hope and trust. Wider peace across North Africa and the Middle East depends on Egypt's stalled progress. What pressure! And yet, extraordinary beauty still flowers among tattered dreams of reform. There is humour and detachment in those I meet. Life, they might as well say, is hard enough as it is – whatever happens, we are still Egyptian!

Of course I'm partial – everything in this country is seen through the lens of my bewitchment. Take Mohammed. He may have the most common Arabic name, but our rapport is anything but ordinary. It certainly didn't spark up straight away. I first spotted him with a stack of towels on the private beach of my hotel. He seemed eager for conversation, managing to engage even the most flaked out of bronzing guests. I imagined a parallel life for him – one with more scope than a job with low wages and long hours. All this I observed incognito, shades on, enjoying my undisturbed solitude. There wasn't much else to do in the afternoon heat. But when he first wandered over to talk to me, I had forgotten my earlier curiosity: iPod on, half asleep – a dreamy interlude between short refreshing swims. I ignored him, as he persisted with a second "Excuse me?" Wasn't it obvious I was unconscious – eyes shut, foetal posture, suncream at the ready, earphones on? "I'm chilling out here," I eventually whispered, with every hint of 'go away' polite restraint can suggest. He got the message. The next day, it was clear he wasn't going to try that again – even though my eyes were open as he walked past, book shut and iPod nowhere to be seen. Without returning my smile, he headed over to the next lounging body in the row of sunbeds. Two days later, when this same routine happened, I was going to take every initiative at conversation.

"Hello. How are you today?" I asked in the ubiquitous tourist rhetoric. It's like the American, 'What's up?' No one expects a considered reply of course. Sometimes, I can't resist indulging a ponderous answer to see how quickly easy smiles become indifferent – "Mmmm, well, now you ask... I'm noticing that..." "How are you?" I ask again.

He stops, looks at me, and lifts up his shades. "I'm good. And you?"

"Very well, thanks. Loving this sun. It's winter at home."

He was in no rush to say anything more. He was short – probably six inches shorter than me. I was lying down so couldn't have really noticed the contrast. It's something that strikes me now, because I have such a strong sense of him physically. I can close my eyes and recall him as if he was right beside me, just as he was then. Was it during that first chat with Mohammed, as he seemed to look at me, really wonder about me, that I noticed another swarm of dragonflies? As the weather turned a few days before, so the dragonflies thrived in fresh pools of rainwater. They thrill me more than any other insect, for their primeval essence unchanged since their first hatch on Earth millions of years ago. They would have been our predators back then; their reptilian striped bodies, intricately patterned wings like skeleton sycamore seeds and glossy-black beaded eyes much larger. On the balcony of my room, two had settled on my left hand, in coitus, forming a perfect swan-necked heart. They stayed like that, a heart pulsing very gently, for some minutes. Witnessing this union felt like a brush with magic.

"I wasn't going to talk to you. After the other day," he declared with beguiling honesty.

"Ah. You mean, the time I was sort of asleep and you tried to talk to me?"

"You were scary," he answered.

"I was relaxed. Crashed out. I'm on holiday!"

He smiled. "I'm glad to speak to you now. You're not what I expected. You seem friendly."

We had somehow navigated through an acknowledged tension, which given our lack of history seemed surprisingly familiar. He read my thoughts. "I'm not like this with everyone by the way! I meet people all the time. But some are different. You get a feeling – and you just know they will be part of your life."

A different day, a different mood, I might have been put off by this intimacy. That day I wasn't. It was the most natural thing, including the assumptions we were at ease enough to make. The next hour was only interrupted with Mohammed scanning the beach, ensuring there was no one needing his attention. At one point he broke off apologetically – to diffuse a flirtation between a glamorous dark Italian woman and her photographing admirer who couldn't speak any English or Italian. The man's bleached mane offset her auburn curls, his tanned toned form and skimpy briefs every bit as bold as her sheer bikini. They were eye-catching: her brazen posing and pouting in the shallows to his enthusiastic encouragements, "Oui, encore, oui!" Neither betrayed concern as Mohammed interrupted their play, pointing out that very strip of beach was only for hotel residents. Yawning, the man reverted his attention to his subject and her giggling approval. More broken English. Did he not understand, Mohammed persisted, this was a private beach? He was not allowed there – time to leave! That way! Mohammed gestured vaguely towards the dusty mountains at the end of the bay.

"What to do?" Mohammed shrugged back at my side, as the snapping resumed. This was part of his job – to protect the exclusivity of this hotel. He soon revealed a keen awareness of beachside dynamics: who was kissing whom, his own more memorable and unlikely fumbles with guests over the years, and fallouts from indiscretions. Nationalities had traits that were quantifiable as far as Mohammed had witnessed. He was a trained psychotherapist, with ambitions for private practice. It was all too clear he was a blatant gossip, with a finely tuned self-awareness – and, what was more, I was hooked by the intrigue conjured by his impressive flow of English. Soon I was thoroughly opened up to the not so private ins and outs of the unsuspecting sunbathers around me.

I had a curious sense of watching my narrow world shapeshift. I too was becoming someone else, enjoying the attention and confidential tones of Mohammed, who was sharing some of his own deepest secrets. "This one," he told me, "no one knows.

Promise me it'll be just you?" I nodded earnestly. I didn't doubt his trust in me for a second. Another time, another life, vivid and nostalgic, animated through his voice: his fiancée's untimely death three years before and the emotional vacuum since. Every passing day, he had remembered their relationship. It was a living hell, he admitted, trying to recapture those feelings of faith in a future now eluding him. As Mohammed spoke, he became more vital – his muscular squatness and sparkling eyes, framed with thick black lashes. It was easy to picture him with a choice of foreign women passing through Dahab. He admitted such encounters left him feeling empty and wretched. "It's all in the feeling." He turned for a moment towards the water. "In the end, I wish it wasn't this way – it's so painful sometimes. But life is pointless without feeling," he added simply.

"Yes. To cut off feelings is to shut out life," I replied, thinking of Grandmother's medicine. Only then could a new, exciting story be lived as it was told – with all the freshness of new beginnings and successive birthdays.

"Surprising, isn't it," he added, replacing his shades. "Who would have thought you, the grumpy person you seemed, would remind me of what it is to be alive – to feel!"

Oh how true that to feel is to live! One afternoon, remembering our conversation, I was struck how Mohammed had understood the core of descent through his own life experience that I was only beginning to live by. Wisdom couldn't be taught – the knocks of life, its disappointments and losses, taught more than any self-help manual or lecture could inspire. I was revisiting a shop in downtown Dahab, for all the wonder it had made me feel when I discovered it. There was the same blazing welcome of dangling lanterns and handmade metal lights, each one a curvaceous work of art. An abundance of curiosities and crafts were arranged in positions for best effect. The very spirit of the shop was like a temple. Its walls were lined with oils, incense, teas and silks, rings and stones, of a quality that elevated browsing to an experience. Nothing looked made in haste purely to be sold. I felt all the rapture of a child who could choose any gift they wanted.

On that second visit, a man had looked up from his work, pliers in hand. An exotic bed of curls crowned his angular face. Not recognising him, I asked if the younger man who'd served me before was about.

"That's my brother," he replied. "Take a seat! You were the one who loved our tea – I'd never heard enthusiasm like it! I make the blend. I've just made some more – sit for another cup!"

I was as surprised by the flawless English as his memory. Usually I'm wary of Egyptian hospitality, because of an unspoken onus of reciprocity: as a ritual of custom, a free tea is usually a prelude to a costly acquisition. "I'm sorry not to remember you from last time," I admitted.

"That's because I was hiding. Look!" He turned around, pointing to a long curtain hanging from a staircase. "That's my secret place. Customers have no idea that when I'm overwhelmed, tired out from a long day, that's where I go – to get away. I hide behind the curtain and the world stops! Tell me, do you hide?"

"Hide? Certainly in my imagination," I laughed, picturing him behind the curtain, lanky and neat.

"It was your voice," he added eagerly. "I sneaked out to take a peek when I heard you speak – going on and on about the tea – the best you'd ever had! It seemed so familiar, your voice, even though we'd never met. Soothing somehow. Different. I had to know who it was! But then you left. I knew we would speak at some point, that you'd be back! And here you are. Welcome!" His eyes were bright with the recognition of a very old friend. "Let's shake hands as strangers would. I'm Mohammed. You?"

"Ah, another Mohammed! Mags."

"Mags is not so ordinary, I think!"

That was the start of a friendship with a man I could have

sworn I'd known forever. An eggcup glass of hibiscus tea with a dash of aniseed and vanilla was refilled as the hours passed. Two years apart, we seemed to understand the surprising twists our lives had taken. Mohammed was divorced, a father of two and had lived in England. One day, back in Dahab, a black whirlwind descended, as he described it, at the peak of his success – so much money, plans for more shops – and crashed him against a sudden rent hike, a drink problem and failing marriage. As he lost his business, all its stock, family and prospects, he despaired his life was ruined and over. The next few years were a blur of drunken nights, brawls, and broken dreams. Then, as he slowly rebuilt his business in a cheaper, more tucked away site, his former landlord took pity and dropped the rent, fed up with a succession of poor tenants. Barely two years since, Mohammed had moved on, working all the hours there were, bar a handful for sleep and seeing his children.

"That's all I do, make stuff. What you see. We don't shut 'til after midnight every day," he said. "This shop brings good luck. Everyone who has worked here becomes a new person. Life gives them a chance to live, not survive but to really live."

"It's true time seems to flow differently here," I agreed. "I felt a magnetism from the moment I walked in. And it drew me back for more!"

We sat silently as a handful of customers came and went, sampling the essential oils, alluringly viscous in the soft glow of lights. Extracting them from plants was an ancient science. I had a cabinet of oils back home, my nose able to sense which one to apply each day.

"Why did it happen?" Mohammed resumed. "Why all that darkness? OK, so I learnt – never to take another day for granted. But did I have to go through all that shit to get the message?"

"Apparently, you did," I answered.

"And you? Why all this being alone – travelling here, going there, doing this, trying that… why are you always choosing to be on your own?"

"I don't know. Maybe, like you, to learn the opposite. I had to go alone, and be alone – to appreciate sharing."

It was true, since my arrival Sinai's vibrant pulse has been nudging me to open up. Despite rising in the night, eager to work, and the solitary hours at my desk, opportunities spring around me. I have to choose which dinner invitation to accept, be alert to surprise encounters when wandering along the beach or exploring Dahab's backstreets. Members of staff fuss about me, as I remain hunched over a laptop all sunny morning and late at night – the man who cleans my room, the one who stocks my fridge, the gardeners, waiters and manager who has tiptoed twice to the edge of my terrace to check if I would run with him along the lagoons.

Each day feels full. I am only here to engage with the simplest rhythm of work, rest and food. There isn't time to snorkel in world-famous reefs nearby, or roam among the canyons. The alien marine worlds have to be imagined rather than experienced. The more productive a day, the more at peace I become. Possibility is in the exquisite harmony of water and desert. The horseshoe lagoons washing against the vast flat sands suggest luck for any heart open enough to receive it. No matter how long I sit, my body feels alive to the extremes of heat and cold promised by the bald peaks framing the peninsula.

One late afternoon, weary with editing, I was closed to such inspiration. A stubborn stasis had gripped me: even fruitless hours at my desk would have to pay off eventually. As my spirits slumped, a throng of hovering birds – like large hummingbirds – flocked among drooping yellow flowers next to my balcony. In a frenzied hum, they feasted among the tree's wispy branches and bell-shaped petals brimming with nectar, as dusky shadows shrank the vista and the temperature dropped. All the while, a satisfying hunger grew in my stomach. The blur of wings, the song of a long journey, soon dissolved my tension.

Did this same magic inspire a bird's egg to drop from the sky and land on me one breakfast? I was finishing an omelette when the egg, a clean emptied half, dropped into my lap. Pondering over the only tree it might have come from – its branches within a few feet of my table – I had to conclude the egg's trajectory from there unlikely, a few feet shy of my lap. Wherever it came from was not so important – for what really mattered was the husk's story of new life hatched.

What of synchronicity – isn't everything a coincidence for anything to happen? Still, in these long, exciting days, simply being awake feels meaningful. My book surprises me with the twists and turns it takes. As I shed the past and the buried feelings within its layers, so I feel lighter. There's a direct return between changing a story with which I was identified, and the spaciousness such transformation inspires. It is like time travelling: events that had seemed chronically disempowering can be filed away as the opportunities they really were. With the clarity of a backward glance, a truer version of what happened emerges. As a 'future self' I am able to articulate a higher, kinder truth for the challenged person I once was. It is possible to become the heroine of every situation that had seemed so crushing in the rapid-fire moment.

Recounting how the uprootedness of exile has played out in my life, its lonely wrench so sad of heart, has shifted my sense of home. The determination of solitary endeavour, the drive to do-do-do, is no longer my defining impulse. There is something sustaining, powerful and brilliant beyond the investment of 'shoulds'. No longer the 'right' side of forty, I can choose to live unapologetically – this is the time, the prime of present: no waiting for something to happen, or for someone important to make it happen for me.

There is no preferable way to be or for circumstances to look. The horizon has nothing in sight to break it up. There is no career, only a manifest absence of life purpose and no one to convince of my raison d'être – least of all myself! After all, I know now I am enjoying untold freedom in not having one.

In the desert's arid, brittle heat, my skin feels as porous as clean sheets of sand. As I swim, sunbathe and indulge varied platters of seafood and mezze, so I celebrate my body as a vehicle for pleasure and discovery. It is made for sensing and experience – alive and vital.

I feel the draw of the full moon. The balmy weather changes. A rising northerly wind tears through the resort. The Internet is down, electricity cut off, every flimsy effort to withstand nature's extremes pointless – especially the volumes of rainwater having to be hoovered away because of the flat outdoor spaces without drainage or run-off. The suction of rainwater managed by a reserve of generators can barely be heard above the unabated wind. Tourists are unable to pass the eruption of tarmac rubble on the way to the airport. The road to Mount Sinai usually overrun with day trippers is also closed. Mysterious forces are at work, my fellow guests exchange, as their eyes feast over the buffet's plentitude.

Each day, I coincide with my three chief allies, windsurfers from Syria, Turkey and Germany. Their spirits soar with every wild gust, after the limp calm days earlier in the week had left them bored and sullen. "We only get out of bed for a gale," one joked. Their faces have darkened in the hammering wind. They're to be my chaperones to Mount Sinai when we can finally get there. I wanted to walk up it beneath a full moon – but cloud and rain would have meant an ascent in snow at altitude. Besides, the road remains impassable. I have to pay my respects to the legendary mountain before I leave, and time is running out for the all-night trip. Perhaps a visit would be unnecessarily literal, I console myself, when Mount Sinai can be felt so clearly with a stilled mind.

The full moon passes and my return home looms. The banter with my erstwhile chaperones continues over successive dinners as we wait for a clear calm night. More exchanges about my writing labours and the thrill of kitesurfing they offer to teach me – perhaps in Turkey if I follow up on their invitation to visit them. Again, they ask me to join them in the bar, and I refuse, knowing I'll be getting up a few hours later to sit at the keyboard.

Grandmother is everywhere. I can feel her in the heat and wind whipping up waves in the shallows, the hail bursting from clouds fringed by the moon's glare – the belching force of the Earth spewing up roads and infrastructure. One local told me he'd never in all his four decades seen such rain. There are reports of snow on the summit of Mount Sinai. I overheard the concierge telling guests it would take several days for the roads to clear. The writing intensifies; time is running out with my imminent departure. Every tension or regret is being honoured in my life's story – the past rising inexorably to be seen and heard, or felt. It is like a wave about to break, unstable and agitating. Could I not take a break, a day off? No such chance! Grandmother is not a containable force. She is waiting for me whether my eyes are open or closed. She is in those who greet me, confide in me, who inspire me to laugh, flirt, resist and share.

There is plenty of light relief to these realisations. Every other day, I have looked forward to emailed updates on the grubby adventures of my dog Rex, from the woman who fostered him as a newly abandoned pup. Lynn is devoted to rehabilitating packs of unloved and sickly dogs, hunting out the best source of bone, mince, toys and training rituals. All these hounds become unlikely heroes in the stories she writes for her grandchildren. I laugh aloud at every episode of the starring Rex, as wilful as he is intelligent. A collie crossed with Jack Russell, his regimen of long, varied walks is necessary for any chance of a semi-mellow evening. Lynn is one of the unforeseen bonuses of Rex bounding into my life to shred slippers and shoes, gnashing through traces of any remaining preciousness.

In a dreamy lull of late afternoon reclined on a sunbed, Rex's impact on my life stands out all the more at this peaceful distance. His survival instinct had won my devotion from the outset – smuggled over the sea from Ireland, to escape death row at an overrun rescue shelter. His fulsome tail-wag and floppy ears are magnetic to children, dog owners, self-confessed cat-is-superior-to-dog triumphalists, surly neighbours, bank clerks, shopkeepers, kind strangers offering to look after him while I visit stores unfettered by his tugs and sniffs. The world opens up wherever we go, and adopting him on the anniversary of St Francis of Assisi, the patron saint of animals, reinforced his gift in my life. I remembered how that first day I was scooping up turd on the green of a local church with all the earnest ceremony of a new dog owner not underwhelmed by responsibilities. In perfect timing, Rex had chosen a spot feet away from a minister putting up a large poster promoting the Saint's blessing the next day, for "all beloved pets, God's animals, large and small."

Such an outing with a new, untrained puppy was undoubtedly ambitious. Among those congregated were a fifty-four year old tortoise, three caged cats, a parrot, large shaggy big-toothed dogs, yapping mutts, dogs a model of well-trained poise, and Rex. The rector put me at my ease as he confided his own Jack Russell was too naughty to be present for the blessing, despite being rewarded recently with Waitrose's finest rump steak after fighting off a burglar.

"Blessed be the animals," he opined, "the meek of heart, the purest souls of all God's beasts, for what they inspire among their human caretakers." A rip of paper drew a row of heads to peer at the ground by my feet, where Rex was devouring a ceremonial programme. "That's enough," I urged telepathically, as prayers and hymns piled up into a cone of paper shreds. For all talk of psychic bonding between pet and owner, Rex and I had work ahead.

Thinking about the populated life I am returning to, to Rex, circles of friends and family, makes languishing in the sun all the more pleasurable. In forging deep, varied connections I am reminded of my own mixed nature. In the two days left in Sinai, I give myself up to a levity of being – my attention drifting as freely as the water lapping along the sand, and breeze that can turn into a gale so suddenly. There is nothing to want, or seek. Every single moment is full enough. The search for more, for meaning, for something to be other than it is, has led me time and again into an unending labyrinth.

Peace, these last two weeks have shown me, is in recreation – the playing with life as the play it is, for the simple reason it feels good this way.

Chapter 18

Into the Stars

It is a vast starry night, and the snort of resting camels makes me jump. It is very cold. Towered over by high canyon walls, my small party trails behind our Bedouin guide towards Mount Sinai. The constellations are bold – the maps of man since wandering began. How strangely insignificant the North Star seems among its bolder rivals, glittering pulses of orange, crimson, magenta, chlorophyll-green and sapphire. My neck cranes like one of the camels at the orchestra of movement and light, the illuminations of ancient time.

The Pleiadian cluster of Seven Sisters is blurred as spilt milk, unlike Orion's belt, the strip of three stars, associated with Osiris, Lord of the Underworld. I had looked up at those same stars forming the God's buckle, with Patrick, outside our hostel at Bugarach. Little did I understand then about one of the most famous mythical descents Osiris had inspired, and the creation story following. After he was hacked into pieces by his jealous brother Seth, his consort Isis was grief-stricken. She dived into the underworld of her despair and then returned, scouring the Nile to recover every piece of him. In putting Osiris back together, Isis literally re-membered him whole. Just like heroines before her and since, she had braved descent and integrated its reclaimed gold: unity.

I scan the sky for the home of Isis – Sirius, the Dog Star. More blue than silver; the most worshipped of all the stars in the sky's temple. Every year, until the Aswan Dam was built, its precise arrival coincided with the Nile's retreat. As Sirius came and went from the skies every six months, so the Nile's rhythm of ebb and flow was as unfailing as a pendulum swing, splitting a year in two. The Nile's flood ensured life sprung improbably from alluvial flats. When it ebbed, the desert regenerated, nutrient-rich and ready for the planting and harvest to follow. Every drop of water would be reclaimed until the farmland was desiccated once more, and the Nile came back, an assurance of life's miracle.

I am somewhere far along from then, cold and comforted by the enclosure of high rock walls. Another snort of a camel. I am so small within the immensity of desert and night sky. Cold stings my cheek the higher we plod. This is the land where Moses encountered the blueprint for the Israelites and their long exodus ahead. The sky is the same sky, the Earth just as solid. Sky and Earth meet, as my throat dries in thirst. We stop for water, only twenty minutes from the top. Here we must wait. I feel biting, numbing cold. I am glad of being here, feeling tired, knowing this relaxing interlude can't go on for much longer.

One of my companions asks me if I'm cold. My lips are blue apparently. I shiver, only aware now of the rigours of such cloudless height. He wraps me in a blanket bartered from the Bedouin who served us tea. It feels good to be snug and hugged within two strong arms. My eyes shut and I start to dream. Gently, I'm nudged awake. The first streak of light beckons us to reach the top for sunrise. Snow crunches beneath our feet – so strange for desert! Our guide thinks so too. He stops to swivel his heel in gritty mush and laughs excitedly.

I step higher, deeper into the hallowed space where Moses heard God's name as: I Am That I Am.

To declare it is to be it, as the creator of my life story. And so, what or who am I, aware of this? Is that you, Grandmother? Is that you in the weight of cold and weariness? What is it that you are, that I am remembering, as you remember me remembered? Are you as much the All, as the Nothing? Is that pointy fuzz of cloud over there to pierce my befuddled mind awake? Was it really a 'you' called Grandmother who made me dive into sensuous descent – to feel myself alive?

I Am That I Am.

Is it you, Grandmother, urging me to open my heart – to the freedom of sweet-nothing in everything outside me? Is that cloud a unicorn's horn, to awaken the crystalline throne and sovereignty within me?

Are you ready to give up all of it – even the separation allowing you to exist?

All of it? What, give up the story of a me, and you? Give up what I see, touch, smell, hear and feel? Do I not need the Weaver to help inspire me to discover a new story – a brighter, more loving, more joy-filled one than that I had been living?

Are you ready to give up the story of the sun and the moon, the stars and galaxies?

Why would I do that, Grandmother? The very force that created the celestial bodies moves through me too. How could I wave away such marvels into the dust?

Flags unfurl, bright banners of colour in the glimmer of dawn. Every spare square foot of rock is crowded with pilgrims. It is a fiesta of languages and songs, chants and chatter, most having waited for days to set foot on Sinai's summit. I am trembling. That is how I know I am not dreaming, that I really am here, cosy in a blanket, experiencing this with so many. The desert starts to come alive, a sea of creases in the dawn. The sun is about to rise. Cameras are poised towards the easterly skyline. I can feel the protective arms of my German friend squeeze me beneath the bristly rug wrapped around us. How lovely to be held, sharing the Sinai vista with another – with all the charge of attraction between us. I Am That I Am. His touch, the curiosity for what might follow when we're off the mountain, the numbing cold, aching weariness, the thrill of contact. Oh what it is to live – to feel!

She asks me to see through the cool lens of detachment – the naked eye witnessing. With no body to experience, without senses to create my world, what else is left? A canvas void of colour, bare, neither beautiful nor barren. No pity or regret. No contrast or embellishment. No drama: no ups and downs, disappointments or triumphs, no what-ifs or thank-goodnesses. No one at the centre of a story called 'me'. Pure being. I Am That I Am.

The sun rises. Thank you, Ra, for another dawn of another day. What lies in the time to come? What sweet freedom to dream myself alive, to dream big, and dream some more! I too hold the light of dawn. All possibility lives within that light, however shadows obscure the un-mined gold buried deep within. In those times of challenge, there is always courage to be claimed among others, together a united force. For stories help us to become the change we seek, as that we already are. Waking up to our power as co-creators of our world, we can inspire a new dream by which the many, not the few, can thrive. When my own concerns become as empty as all the others, how might I serve a new collective story, its heart-centred intent an unstoppable force to make a fractured, violent world a better place? I am only waking up now to the tender invitation of descent: to follow heartbreak and passion as the way of bliss.

Whatever you may think, there has never been and never can be any separation between inner and outer, Self and Other. The warring mind has forgotten. The peaceful self is remembering all that has been and all that could never have really been. Before then, you didn't exist – you only thought you did. Telling your story re-informs the collective memory of the One Mind that we are... remembering!

Oh, Grandmother, must I really give up all this – including your fierce love? I'm having way too much fun with my attachments, even when I think I'm not, forgetting again how much I love to think I'm wronged, pained or in doubt.

And out there within the brightening horizon I know is unending life and death. What, who with and where next? Laughter and sharing, joy, tears and rage. When I forget there is such a choice as the storyteller I am, there is the wink of Grandmother to recall, and Rex's muddy-pawed leap on me, reminding me I'm never really alone, for some things never change. Whatever happens, I will always love, as I too am loved, just as much anyway. At some point in the muddle, fear and doubt, I am bound to wake up – again – to remember there is only one of us really here, making up this whole fiction called life.

Epilogue

Rex and I pound along fields of dried mud tracks towards the sea. As he runs, his Jack Russell ears pinned back in motion seem ludicrously sweet, like furry wings, inspiring me to shriek as I pointlessly try to overtake, "Rexie Roo!" My voice sounds so childish – but I can't help expressing what rises in me. It's close to dusk and the fields are glowing a soft red. Coconut, the rich sweetness of flowering gorse, wafts out from along the field's edge. I stop still and inhale it – spicy and moist – exotic in the familiar farmland where I grew up.

The shrill gabble of geese gets louder as they approach, heading inland – only two at first, curiously heavy as birds known for their airborne grace over vast distances. They pass directly above and circle, wings beating like the throb of a soft drum, returning this time with hundreds of others. They get lower and glide over me as one mass. Each one's cry is distinctive and urgent. Aware of my shallow breathing, I take a slow deep breath. And another. I know they're going to land in my field. Instead they fly on, thrilling and powerful, before doubling back like an afterthought.

A particularly rackety goose breaks away from the flank, and dives to the ground. The whole flock follows, swooping and settling as one wing. A scattering of crows watches among the stumps of burnt corn an audience. The goose chorus stops. The silence has such an active quality – so much charge in it – as I too watch, Rex at my feet. I am touched by beauty, but there's more to my excitement than that. What speaks to me is of another story, as much about descending as the long flight to touch down, each flock member essential to its arrival. The grounding goose evokes very different terrain in me from its voyaging instinct – for I know about descent: choosing to give up the peaks of aspiration and venture in the opposite direction. For all the challenge such a journey demands, there has been immeasurable freedom in forsaking the story of tomorrows, dropping into the vibrant real world of physical experience.

Stillness settles over the field. And my heart lifts, comforted – recognising the peace when motion stops, when the unrest summoning a long journey ends – even for a moment – or until the next hint of sunlight, the dawn of another day. Rex looks up at me. I pat him. If we press on for another couple of fields, there's a short cut home winding back along the river. I feel so very alive: this is peace. This is what it is to arrive. And I can only know this because it hasn't always been this way.

Ten Wisdoms of Descent
Inspired by Grandmother

1. Feel – I Am alive

2. Breathe consciously – I Am present

3. Dream big – I Am possibility

4. Give up judgment – I Am acceptance

5. Live each day as the last – I Am courage

6. Heal inner conflict – I Am peace

7. Dance – I Am celebration

8. Co-create – I Am united

9. Be the change – I Am the world

10. Open the heart – I Am love

For more information about the author
Mags MacKean, her talks, workshops and guided
journeys: www.magsmackean.com

BOOKS

O is a symbol of the world, of oneness and unity; this eye represents knowledge and insight. We publish titles on general spirituality and living a spiritual life. We aim to inform and help you on your own journey in this life.

Visit our website: http://www.o-books.com

Find us on Facebook:
https://www.facebook.com/OBooks

Follow us on Twitter: @obooks